DOESN'T LIVE HERE
ANYMORE

ALSO BY BARB OWEN

NORMAL Doesn't Live Here Anymore
is also available on all popular **eBook** readers and as an
audio-book, read by the author, Barb Owen.

Purchase your eBook or Audio Book copy at:
http://www.HopeForCaregivers.com/giftshop

Merchandise: Be sure to buy some of the wonderful items that
were inspired by the writing of this book, to name a few:

- ❀ Coffee Table Book of original artwork from the pages
  of **Normal Doesn't Live Here Anymore**

- ❀ "Ooh La La!" coffee & tea mug

- ❀ "Time for ME TIME!" Sweatshirts and T-Shirts

- ❀ "Hope Calendar" full of encouraging messages

HopeForCaregivers.com is designed to support and encourage
caregivers. Along with blog entries by the author, you'll
find resources and suggestions for navigating through the
caregiving experience. Each caregiving journey is individual,
but one need unites all—the need for hope—hope that you
make good decisions—hope that you will stay healthy—hope
that life will somehow get back to normal—and most of all,
hope that you can get from one day to the next.

HopeForCaregivers.com exists for YOU, to give you HOPE.

Please come by and say hello. You are always welcome!

NORMAL

DOESN'T LIVE HERE ANYMORE

AN INSPIRING STORY OF HOPE FOR CAREGIVERS

BARB OWEN

Daniel Boone
Regional Library

T&TI inc.

Columbia, Missouri

Published in the United States by: T&T1 inc., P.O. Box 30716, Columbia MO 65205-3716
Phone (573) 723-1510 • www.HopeForCaregivers.com • contact@HopeForCaregivers.com

Editorial supervision: Race Owen
Design: Race Owen

Library of Congress Cataloging-in-Publication Data

Owen, Barb
Normal Doesn't Live Here Anymore : An Inspiring Story of Hope for Caregivers / Barb Owen
    p. cm.
ISBN 13: 978-1456474294 (trade pbk.) 10: 1456474294 (trade pbk.)
1. Caregiving. 2. Self Help. 3. Inspirational. 4. Eldercare. I. Owen, Barb. II. Title.

2010919426

Tradepaper ISBN 13: 978-1456474294
Tradepaper ISBN 10: 1456474294

01 03 05 07 09   10 08 06 04 02
1st printing, 2011

Published in the United States of America

"I can be changed by what happens to me.
I refuse to be reduced by it."

– Maya Angelou

***

This book is dedicated to
my husband, my friend
my son, my best

Thank you both for your love, support and
unbelievable patience.

***

CONTENTS

PART II: REGROUP, RECOGNIZE, REBIRTH 193

PART III: HINDSIGHT, HEALTH, HOPE   367

PROLOGUE

One January, four of us began having dinner together every month. It was finally **our** time. All of our kids were grown, living productive lives and no longer needed our daily interaction. The future had arrived and we could actually concentrate on the lives we'd always dreamed about. None of us were quite sure what might happen next, but we instinctively knew one thing; we needed to cultivate good friends.

As we enjoyed our monthly meals, we talked about our occupations, hobbies and families as well as our physical changes, and compared the way our mothers' bodies had begun to emerge in our own reflections. Month by month a closeness beyond description knitted our hearts together as Soul-Sisters.

After several years, the unthinkable happened. One of us became ill. Several months later we heard the diagnosis — cancer. Friendship evolved into activity, assisting her family in any way we could — meals, transportation to chemo treatments, thinking up ways to positively distract our friend's attention, going with her to select her new wig, sewing special hats — and anything else we could think of to put a smile on her face while trying to avoid what appeared to be the inevitable. In spite of our best efforts, cancer stole her from all of us.

It was nearly unbearable.... our first meal together as we faced the empty chair where our fourth Soul-Sister was supposed to be sitting... Ignoring the vacancy and the deafening silence was impossible. Instead, the tears welled up in our eyes, not only for the profound loss of our friend, but also for each love-filled journey and loss we had endured over a five year stretch. Those years bonded us for life as we bore witness to the loss of eight people, including our parents and in-laws, as well as our dear friend.

One by one, circumstances beyond our control caused each of us to become a caregiver. Accepting the new responsibility, without any preparation, meant leaning heavily on each other as each of us had been given the primary responsibility for our loved ones. None of us had experience being caregivers. None of us knew what to do first. None of us knew about the necessity of self-care.

We were the epitome of deer caught in the headlights when "caregiver" became synonymous with each of our names. Barb was the first in our group to experience the loss of a family member. One by one, our losses followed closely behind hers.

Through our shared experiences, we discovered how emotions ebbed, flowed, and at times, even disappeared. We encouraged each other to feel what we felt without judgment. Sometimes it made no sense to feel sad, angry, grief-stricken, or guilty. And, the over-arching feeling that superseded everything was a longing to get back to a normal life. Every time we met as soul-sisters, we brushed the edges of normal. Every time we shared a meal together, we felt almost normal again. Each time one of us said, "I understand," and meant it , the crazy one felt a little less crazy.

Time has passed. Our lives changed forever. And yes, we each found normal again - a new normal - a new balance - a richer life as "caregiver" was etched into a facet of our personalities. Oh how we wish we'd had this book to assist us with the journeys that none of us really understood at the time. The insights in **Normal Doesn't Live Here Anymore** would have made our individual experiences less confusing and overwhelming.

Brew a pot of tea, curl up in your favorite chair and embrace the words that come from years of one caregiver's experience. Barb allows you to walk with her—step by step—through her caregiving journey as she weaves her story along with her hindsight, questions you need to ask, information you will need, and the emphatic necessity for Me Time.

Someone once said, "Friends are the family we would have chosen for ourselves." We hope you will follow our example and create your own special family. Wholeheartedly we can say, "You need your friends!" There is a bond that connects caregivers everywhere. As you read this book we're sure that you will feel that circle expand to include you. Starting right now, we embrace you. Welcome to the circle!

As friends who have "been there and done it" we salute you. We honor you. We wish you clarity and peace on your journey.

Now, grab that cup of tea and a few minutes, take a few deep breaths and join Barb on a journey of love, compassion, sorrow, and encouragement.

— With love, The Soul-Sisters

PREFACE

The world as I knew it had collapsed into chaos, leaving my emotions in a tangled mess. Wandering without clarity from one day to the next, I picked up a pen and began writing. It was a way of remembering, and an attempt to remove the incessant chatter from my head. Even as the foggy days of caregiving were playing out in front of me, I discovered that fatigue fathered forgetfulness. I was terrified that I would allow exhaustion to cloud my memories and felt compelled to write everything in the notebook I kept with me. Writing a book was the farthest thing from my mind. Survival and remembering were my only goals.

After several years of noting events and feelings, the notebook of thoughts seemed to take on a life of its own and evolved into the idea for this story. My mother read the original draft when it was about 75% completed. Her response, "Thank you so much for writing this. I'd forgotten so many things about our journey together." And she went on to say, "You should let other people read this. I like it!"

With Mom's approval and encouragement, you are holding that story in your hands.

DEAR READER

When thrown into the role of caregiver, life often becomes surreal, careening out of control. Perhaps you are embarking on your own caregiving journey, without the benefit of experience and preparation. As you read my story, I have included a practical reflection—a bit of wisdom gained from experience—after each chapter, extending hope and allowing you to apply something from my journey to your own. I don't pretend to have all the answers regarding caregiving, so this book is not a ***how to***, but rather a story based around my experience.

Please note that names and some details have been changed throughout the story.

I wish you stamina and peace as you navigate your role as caregiver.

Blessings, Barb

INTRODUCTION

I t's only 10 o'clock in the morning and the familiar fatigue has already arrived. I've prepared breakfast and lunch for my husband and managed to swallow a few bites of food between trips up the steps to care for my mother. So far today I've made sure that she had breakfast, dealt with bedside commode issues, washed multiple loads of laundry including sheets, towels, and clean up rags, given Mom a shower, dressed her and made sure that she's comfortable and contented, hopefully for a few hours.

An unending list scrolls through my brain… grocery store… pharmacy… doctors' appointments… don't forget Mom's hair and nail appointments… plan meals… make a sandwich for Mom and loosen the cap on the Ensure bottle so she can "open it herself" at lunch time… fold all the clean laundry… run the vacuum cleaner… dust the furniture… clean the bathrooms… spend time with Mom… feed the animals… relax… take a quick nap… deal with the piles of bills and bank statements… balance the checkbook… take a bath and put on fresh clothes… always be prepared for the unexpected… check the schedule to see who stays with Mom tonight… and try not to borrow trouble… live in the moment… this moment… one moment at a time…

As I catch myself staring out the window I notice that Spring has begun to emerge from a seemingly endless winter. It's been colder and snowier than in past years and I wonder when the daffodils, hyacinths, and forsythia began blooming.

The past few years are blurred as a spiral of despair threatens to pull me downward. My spirit, fading to grey and withering beneath the weight of responsibility, somehow hears a tiny voice whispering, "Writing can heal."

As I listened and remembered, the story began to spill onto countless journal pages.

What we call despair is often only the painful eagerness of unfed hope.

– George Eliot

PART 1

BIRTH
BEWILDERED
BIDDING ADIEU

REFLECTION

JUST HANG ON

I n spite of the appearance of everything falling apart... in spite of not recognizing yourself anymore... in spite of feeling completely disoriented, you can **hang on**. If you **hang on**, the sun will rise again tomorrow and you can see the beauty of spring flowers, a symbol of hope.

You don't know what to do, yet a tiny voice inside whispers, **"Hang on. You can do it."** Just being able to hear that voice is reassuring.

Sometimes you have to ask someone stronger than yourself to help because you, alone, no longer have the strength. You could even write the words, *Hang On*, on sticky notes and put them on the mirror or refrigerator. Stick them in lots of places so you see them often. There is power hidden in these words.

I'm sure the blooms waiting safely within frozen bulbs somehow know that if they just hang on, they will eventually feel the warmth of the sun, allowing them to finally grow. I hope you can accept encouragement from the blooms and little by little, you'll find that hanging on isn't so difficult. Little by little you will store those words in your heart, not just on a mirror.

Just like the blooms hidden within the bulbs, please know that warmth and light are within reach.

Today, know that you can hang on.

CHAPTER 1

LIFE BEFORE

I came into the world as the baby of my family. My mother repeatedly told me how much my four older sisters adored *their* new baby and how they voted me into the family. Every month Mom and Dad held family council meetings in order to distribute everyone's spending money, announce rule changes, and anything else important to the family. The meetings were complete with a president, vice-president and secretary who took notes in special books reserved only for family council details. Their gatherings were also an opportunity for my parents to demonstrate proper etiquette and *Robert's Rules of Order*. At just such a meeting, the thirteen-year-old politely raised her hand and upon recognition began to speak. "Well, the rest of the girls and I have been talking and we've decided that we need another baby in this family. So, I make a motion that we do that, okay?"

Speechless and searching for a response, Mom and Dad just looked at each other.

Realizing her opportunity, the ten-year-old's hand shot up and without waiting to be acknowledged, she blurted out, "I second the motion! Let's have a baby! We *need* one! All in favor say 'Aye'!"

The enthusiastic chorus from the mouths of four girls, ages seven to fifteen, snapped my parents back into the moment, just in time for my dad to regain order, pound the gavel, and in a booming voice declare, "Your mother and I say NO! We *do not* need any more babies!" Including my mom in the veto stretched the truth just a bit, because honestly, my mother would have enjoyed having babies forever. Being a mother was her sole identity, and she wasn't sure what to do with her empty arms.

In spite of the parental overruling, my sisters received their wish and I arrived a few months later, exactly eight years after my parents' *last baby*.

Wonderful memories float through my mind about our years at home, together. Christmas, like so many other holidays, was especially magical. Each year I found a new doll under the tree, until my parents decided that I had outgrown such a childish tradition, even though I never really outgrew it!

Dad's camera, continually poised to capture formal photos as well as any embarrassing moment, provided countless opportunities we all loved to relive and laugh about later. Some of my favorite pictures show all of us girls with new Easter dresses, sewn by Mom, and beautiful fresh-flower headbands, created by Dad, pinching our temples until they ached. No matter how much my head hurt, I loved feeling like a princess, offering my best smile for the camera, as I savored the sweet perfume of the flowers floating around my head.

Dad enjoyed showing off his ability with flowers anytime. Anything dealing with flowers, including teaching students as a professor of floriculture, building new gardens and speaking to garden clubs, occupied most of Dad's life. A wife and five daughters were always proud to model his showy corsages and other creations. Dad's snapshots, now housed in photo albums, still instantly transport me back to the happy memories of my sisters and the time we spent together as a family.

By the time I was ten years old, all of my sisters were gone from home and I missed them terribly. The house, once alive with girls' giggling, arguing, and whispered secrets, became strangely silent and I was left alone with my gray-haired parents. School activities occupied me, while marriages and babies consumed my sisters. The age differences between me and the others never allowed real connection, no matter how much I yearned for it. I always wanted to be a part of their lives and to be included, but common ground was difficult for any of us to find. I so wanted them to see me as something other than their pesky "little sister."

After graduating from high school and attending college, my adult life began at age nineteen when I married an amazingly talented, supportive man. He was ten years my senior and recently widowed. His daughter from a previous marriage was almost eleven years old at the time of our wedding. I was not much more than a child myself, yet I had no doubt about being a mother. It just didn't appear to be that hard! After all, I had watched my mother survive raising five daughters, so I could surely help one little girl get through the next few years of growing up. I was lost in my exuberant fantasy of sewing for a daughter, teaching her about things that I enjoyed and listening to her discoveries about life. I was certain she would love me and everything I wanted to teach her.

Six days before my twenty-second birthday I gave birth to our son, the true light of my life. From the instant that he came into this world, I was in love. Only an occasional moment during his childhood and life at home caused me self-doubt about parenting. Raising a little boy proved to be a challenge from time to time, as my only frame of reference came from living around girls. On the other hand, being a step-parent proved to be a monumental challenge as I found replacing my stepdaughter's mother was not well received much of the time. Overcoming preconceived notions about wicked stepmothers, purported in books and by not-so-well-meaning relatives, added to the challenge of successful step-parenting. In spite of the ups and downs, we all survived our first ten years together. When my stepdaughter left for college, I believed that I had passed through the most difficult season of my life. Oh, the blissful ignorance of youth!

In addition to being a wife and mother, I have always been an enthusiastic life-long student and teacher. Whatever I learned, I eventually taught—a passion I discovered at age sixteen when I began teaching piano lessons on the spinet in my bedroom. I loved teaching as well as performing. Watching and listening to my students as they progressed from beginners to confident musicians, thrilled me. As a performer I learned very complex compositions that I played alone or in ensemble with a partner. Sometimes we enjoyed the challenge of four hands on one piano and other times, performed on two beautiful concert grands. Early in my life I realized that music brought me comfort, yet also diffused intense emotions. Anger or sadness could send me straight to the bench to play until the disagreeable feelings dissolved. And then it would happen...JOY... soul-joy... and I remembered the real reason for my music. It was mine and **I loved it!**

I found the art of decorative painting when my son was a toddler. Once a week my mother eagerly spent time with him, allowing me a couple of hours for myself. Through the use of drawn patterns I studied the way shadow and light as well as tints, tones and shades of color could create objects with dimension. Occasionally I would even try to draw something myself, although my inner critic rarely approved. After several years of honing my skills in classes, my friends asked me to teach them and my passion for teaghing was once again fueled as I loved watching people discover joy and satisfaction in the painting process.

Dolls occupied much of my life and imagination from the time I was a tiny girl. Learning to stitch simple blankets and doll clothes with my mother, ignited my love of sewing. Time simply evaporated when I sewed and dressed my collection of dolls. As my sewing skills developed, I sewed evermore elaborate dresses, including an entire wedding scene, for my fashion doll. All the hours of designing and pretending filled some of the emptiness left behind by my sisters. When they came home to visit, my sisters thought my creations were pretty silly until they saw how I designed and stitched my own wedding dress and those of my attendants, saving lots of money!

Many years later while perusing a catalog, I stumbled upon a book about making cloth dolls and a new idea was born: I could create dolls myself! I knew I could sew the clothing and accessories, but could I design the actual doll's body, too? Seeking inspiration, my discovery of the new phenomena of online communities connected me to doll makers all over the world. I found limitless resources, as well as answers for my questions without ever leaving my desk.

Doll making evolved easily into teaching, first on the local level and then into a classroom without walls—the Internet. What a transforming experience—students all over the world learning from me without a physical classroom! My passion for teaching exploded and I built a thriving design business that further supported my classes. With help and encouragement from my husband, I created my own line of patterns and rubber stamps, and expanded my business from retail into wholesale. In early 1999, one year after developing my new business, in a casual conversation with an associate, she remarked that someone needed to write a book about a specific doll making technique. Intrigued, I began exploring the possibility of writing just such a book, enabling me to teach in a whole new way.

REFLECTION

PASSION

Take a moment and look back. Do you notice a recurring theme in your life? What has fueled your existence so far? What has made life worth living? What adds color to your life?

The color... life-fuel I call it, is **Passion**. Without it, life fades into shades of gray and becomes little more than an act of wandering from one day to the next. If you are lucky enough to have discovered more than one **Passion**, be ever so grateful, as one may sustain you during a difficult period when another has been extinguished.

What happens when your **Passion** has been stomped out by overwhelming responsibilities?

When the crescendo of stress threatens to crush you, how can you go on?

Begin with one simple choice. So much in life begins with a choice. We never lose the power to choose, even if the only choice you have is your attitude about something or someone. So, here's a chance to do just that. Choose to kindle an ember of **Passion**. Even if you choose to try for only a few minutes today, the ember may glow a bit. Tomorrow, vow to fan that tiny ember again. And, the next day choose to give it more attention.

And then a discovery! **Passion** is not lost, but rather waiting, patiently. It was there all the time.

Today, you can not only hang on, you can remember your passion and embrace it again.

CHAPTER 2

A FULL HEART

After spending the summer months absorbed by the writing process, the doll making book became a reality. Putting my energy into writing helped diffuse my overpowering emotions as I anticipated our son, now grown, preparing to leave the safety and familiarity of home.

Simultaneously, my aging parents were needing additional attention which resulted in them absorbing larger and larger blocks of my time. Within me I could feel a dormant rebellion stirring. I loved and respected my parents, but I couldn't help recalling their disdain from long ago when I married. They vehemently disagreed with my choice of husbands who was, "too old and only wanted me to take care of his daughter." They were so opposed to him, that my father refused to escort me down the aisle and made certain that I understood their disapproval with his conversation and letters. When my parents finally appeared at our wedding, I saw their choice of seats—the back pew. I was their last child to marry, but they chose the back row in the church to put an exclamation point on their aversion to my action.

Reflecting on my parents' appearance that day, I suppose that

I should have been able to give them the benefit of the doubt as they had buried their second-born daughter, killed in a car accident, only a few months before my wedding. Their grief convinced them that when I married someone other than their choice, they would be losing another daughter. Our marriage was still strong after more than thirty years, but reliving my parents' rejection of long ago still stung. Struggling with their increasing dependence, I experienced conflicting emotions every time they needed me. I wanted to reject them as they had rejected me, yet somehow I couldn't. My conscience convinced me to set aside the old anger and wounds as best I could. I knew that none of us could go back to hit the *re-do* button, and I certainly didn't want to spend the time I had left with my son swallowed up by resentment toward his grandparents.

In late October, 2000, our son began his journey from the Midwest to California. I rode with him in his classic Mustang as far as a friend's home in Colorado and then through a flood of tears, bid him good-bye and Godspeed. To see him drive away was nearly more than my heart could bear. For my only son to find the courage and self-confidence to build his life in a place completely unknown to him, filled me with myriad emotions. I was elated by his courage to pursue his dream, followed quickly by my fear of the future and a longing for those years when his tiny hand always found its way into mine. I could barely take it in. All the years... all the feelings... all the love... Everything was acute and unfocused in the same instant, punctuated by the searing pain in my heart as I watched him leave.

But, the clock never turns back and watching **my best** launch into adulthood, without looking back at me, happened whether I was ready or not.

In a full heart there is room

for everything...

– Antonio Porchia

REFLECTION

MIXED EMOTIONS

Emotions are funny things. It's possible to feel something so strongly that you can't imagine its intensity will ever lessen. The feeling rolls over and over in your heart, demanding all of your attention. And it's possible to feel nothing at all. Empty... void... blank... Amazingly, it's also possible to feel opposites at the very same time!

Well-meaning people may try to convince you that only certain emotions have value. Sometimes they even label the way you feel as **good** or **bad**. And you may even do that to yourself. If you're not alert to the danger of emotion-labeling, you may succumb to an illusion that tricks you into thinking you cannot identify or trust what you feel.

The Truth is that every emotion is absolutely valid and holds its own lesson. Being the amazing humans that we are, we can feel multiple and seemingly opposing feelings at the same time! How little sense that seems to make and how very confusing. But contained within simple acceptance is freedom.

You are free to feel exactly what you feel. There is no **good** or **bad**, no **right** or **wrong**. **Feel what you feel**. Express it by talking or writing or just sit in the mix of your feelings, whether exhilarating or debilitating or in between. Simply recognize emotions for what they are—teachers. In time you will learn their lessons. For now, there is no need to rush into understanding.

Just feel what you feel.

Nobody has ever measured, not even poets,

how much the heart can hold

– Zelda Fitzgerald

CHAPTER 3

CHANGES AT HOME

U pon returning home from the trip with our son, I learned that my parents had slipped significantly further down the slope of aging while I was away. One of my sisters, *SANCTIMONIOUS SHIRLEY*, (who knew best about everything because of her perceived extra special God-hotline) had planned one of her brief rare visits in their home. Her intention had been to leave after just a few days, but as Dad was ailing, she extended her stay until I returned. Mild discomfort had evolved into constant pain and Dad was miserable.

SANCTIMONIOUS SHIRLEY, usually piously quiet, left long winded messages on my answering machine about our parents' situation, including her opinion about the cause of Dad's symptoms.

"I need you to go to the copy store and pick up the pages of information that my husband is faxing to us. He has spent hours researching one of Dad's prescription drugs that we are certain is causing his problems. With my husband's extensive chemistry background, I'm sure that he is correct in his conclusion about this situation."

Not leaving my mother out of the equation, SANCTIMONIOUS SHIRLEY continued, "Mother is not doing that well either. She's getting weaker and I'm noticing that simple tasks are sometimes well beyond her comprehension or ability. Each time I see her she is more confused, but Dad's issues seem to have somehow propelled her into being nearly immobilized. This situation is getting worse by the day. Dad is becoming more impatient with Mom as her confusion increases and Mom doesn't understand why he is so short with her."

Nowhere in my sister's plethora of observations about Mom and Dad did she bother to ask me, "How are you?" My entire life had changed in ten days. Emptiness occupied the space where my son had been and his room was suddenly void of his spirit as well as his possessions. From the day my sister left home at the age of 21, she required understanding from me that she couldn't help with our parents because any situation in her own family superseded the needs of everyone else. I was expected to acknowledge and accept the black and white instructions God delivered regarding her responsibility and priorities. She showed no compassion for the sudden shift in my world and dismissed my aching soul as an unimportant personal issue. Instead, upon my return home, it was understood that I would immediately assume the role of designated problem solver for our parents.

The papers from SANCTIMONIOUS SHIRLEY'S HUSBAND were filled with technical jargon that no one could understand except Dad's physician. Talking with the doctor was hopeless because he was the one who prescribed the medication, and Dad would never question his doctor. My dad was part of the generation that revered anyone with education greater than his own which translated into unwavering trust and acceptance that a doctor would never give him something that could hurt him.

Frustrated, with no cooperation from Dad, SANCTIMONIOUS SHIRLEY decided to go home, just as EXHAUSTED TERESA (my outspoken, but ever-fatigued sister) arrived. As she was prone to do, EXHAUSTED TERESA asked our parents a couple of questions, drew her own conclusions and continued a laundry list of instructions for me.

EXHAUSTED TERESA's opinions trumped anyone in conversation, but her smile and infectious laugh somehow softened her tone and could draw most anyone to her point of view. Her years of being an award-winning top salesperson boosted her opinion that she was right far more often than she was wrong, making any sort of communication with her a challenge. All my sisters lived less than a two-hour drive away from our parents, but this distance gave each of them permission to insist that I, being the in-town daughter, was to be "responsible for our parents." An infrequent trip home gave each of my sisters an inflated strength of wisdom and power to observe. Certainly, there had been occasions when an extra set of eyes and ears proved helpful. This time, however, in spite of my shattered heart, my sisters were not only unwilling to give me any space, they were extremely annoyed by my lack of communication with them. I needed time to grieve the profound change in my life and to grasp the plight of my parents, not a committee meeting with my sisters where they doled out opinions that always felt more like orders.

A few days after *EXHAUSTED TERESA'S* arrival, Dad's pain worsened significantly and she decided to take him to the emergency room. *EXHAUSTED TERESA* phoned repeatedly, leaving messages on my answering machine, because she wanted me to go with them to the hospital. I assumed that she was capable of dealing with the situation, so I took an afternoon for myself. Every fiber of my being recognized that as soon as *EXHAUSTED TERESA* left, the task of caring for our parents would fall in my lap. Dad's emergency room visit resulted in a diagnosis of Polymyalgia and a prescription for steroids. As soon as she returned home with Dad, *EXHAUSTED TERESA* phoned me and elaborated about her disappointment with me for not being more supportive of our parents and chastised me for leaving her alone to deal with everything. After enduring her verbal lashing, I asked what the doctor said about dad.

"If you had been with us, you could have heard that for yourself, you know." My sister continued, "We saw the doctor on call and he said that he wasn't absolutely certain of Dad's condition, but explained that the new medication should impact his pain level quickly. If it doesn't, he will have to undergo additional testing. All the doctor really did was send Dad back home with paperwork and a prescription that now I have to go to the pharmacy to get filled."

EXHAUSTED TERESA droned on about our parents, complaining about Dad's attitude, Mom's incompetence and insisted that something be done about their situation. Clearly, my sister only wanted to rehash Mom and Dad's increasing needs. She expressed the same concerns repeatedly with different adjectives, just in case I missed the importance of her opinion. Worn down by EXHAUSTED TERESA's words, I decided it was time to speak with our parents. Although EXHAUSTED TERESA was still physically present in their home, to me she was irrelevant. She would be going back to her home in a neighboring state, leaving the blanket of responsibility for our parents resting on me.

Late in the afternoon I arrived at our parents' home, and found my dad reclining in his favorite chair. After kissing his forehead, I asked, "How are you feeling?"

"Not much different," he sighed, heavily.

"I thought the emergency room doctor said that with the medication, you would be getting some relief from the pain by now. Do you think we need to call him?" I asked.

Seeing my confusion, my father said, "I don't have the prescription yet."

The emergency room ordeal occurred in the early morning hours. It was now 5:00 p.m., nearly ten hours later, and the prescription, meant to give fast-acting relief, had yet to be filled?

My sister, seeing a crimson flush crawling up my neck, quickly explained, "I was just getting ready to go to the pharmacy to fill the prescription. You couldn't possibly understand how exhausting and stressful this day has been! I could barely move by the time we got home from the hospital. What an awful place to have to go!"

For a moment, I simply stared at my sister. Then I looked at my dad's sad, pain-laden eyes. Mystified by my sister's selfishness, shock quickly escalated into anger as I tried to comprehend her words and attitude.

Seething in utter disbelief, I turned from my sister and focused on my parents.

After a deep breath I said, "While she goes to get your medication, I think we need to talk for a few minutes. I have a couple of questions for you."

Mom slowly walked into the living room and with the aid of her new lift-chair, lowered herself to the same level beside my dad. I chose a seat across from them where I might observe their reactions to our discussion. My self-centered, exhausted sister apparently forgot her intention to go to the pharmacy and moved a chair as close as she dared.

I never anticipated being in such an uncomfortable position and tried not to fidget as I said, "Taking care of everything around here seems kind of overwhelming for you both now. I think we may need to make some adjustments to give you a little extra help. What do you think?"

EXHAUSTED TERESA interjected, "Oh yes, they need help! You just have no idea how much help is needed around here!"

Ignoring her in order to maintain my rapidly diminishing composure, I looked at my parents and waited for a response.

After a moment of contemplation my dad answered, "Yes, I think your mother could use some help with laundry, changing bed linens, bathing, and maybe a few other things." That was my dad! He was the one who had been in the emergency room that day, but my mom was the one who needed help! Gently asking questions and listening to their answers, the somewhat awkward conversation continued and Mom and Dad's greatest desire emerged.

Dad looked at my mom and then at me. After a moment of silence he said,

"We just want to stay in our own home as long as possible. What has to happen so we can do that?"

Willing myself to speak I said, "I'm not sure, but I think we can figure it out."

Armed with the tablet of notes I'd taken during our conversation, I prepared to leave. Glancing at my sister, I suggested that she might finally go pick up Dad's medication. She grabbed the car keys, stuffed her arms into her sweater and muttered under her breath, "You think you know everything that's going on around here. You know absolutely nothing because you're never here!" And before I could respond, she walked out and shut the door behind her with just enough force to make sure that I understood her point.

After a moment I said, "Well, I'll get to work on this list and figure things out, beginning on Monday. Dad, let's see how your night goes and how you're feeling tomorrow. Keep me posted."

"Thank you so much for coming over. We love you," said Dad. Mom, consumed by her own fears, nodded in agreement as tears teetered on the edge of her eyelids. After embracing each of my parents and assuring them that I would do everything possible to honor their wishes, I left.

As I drove home, a fog of fatigue settled around me as I thought about what steps had to be taken to keep my parents safe and comfortable at home. The seeds of anxiety began to sprout as I drove toward my house. I wondered how I would ever figure out what to do. I wondered why finding help was my job. I wondered what was in store for all of us. And most of all, I wondered what might happen if I weren't successful in my search.

My instincts accurately predicted that the shape of our lives had shifted. Joy began leaking from my soul as I faced the possibility that none of us might ever know **normal** again.

I have to remind myself to breathe—

almost to remind my heart to beat.

– Emily Brontë

REFLECTION

LISTEN

Too many times we talk, rattling on with a personal agenda. Or we dither away trying to conjure up a solution for a real or imaginary problem. Seldom is the first choice to **listen**. We seem to think that beating a subject to death with words will somehow present a magic answer.

When talking proves fruitless, stop and listen.

Examine, just for a moment, who might be important to listen to. Do you need to listen to another person—perhaps a doctor, family member, pastor, or friend? Do you need to listen to that too often ignored inner voice? Do you need to listen to someone that you can't see— someone who isn't covered in skin?

If you find yourself caring for another person for a temporary or an extended period, one of your best assets is the ability to listen. Resources and answers abound if you close your mouth and open your ears. It's absolutely amazing what you can learn when you stop talking!

Just listen.

ഇ ഇ 🍂 ഇ ഇ

CHAPTER 4

BEGINNING

The process of beginning to take control of someone's life is not pleasant. Even though my parents admitted the need for assistance in order to stay in their own home, they were not anxious to have outsiders intrude in their lives. Especially my mother would have been quite happy to have me, and only me, fill her days. Instinctively I knew that I must explore options beyond myself.

Monday morning dawned, ushering in the search for help for my parents. If they were to stay at home, they would need help—lots of help, I thought. I began leafing through the phone book yellow pages. One phone call led to another. Referrals and multiple lists filled my notebook as I began exploring various possibilities. Time seemed to speed up as many options confused me.

EXHAUSTED TERESA, after staying with Mom and Dad for a few more days, decided to go back to her own life leaving behind little doubt about her intention to avoid involvement in our parents' lives, if possible. Always reminding anyone who would listen, she droned on and on about how difficult and tiring it was to be with our parents. Catching me alone, in spite of my efforts to dodge her, my sister grabbed the opportunity to complain, "I am completely worn out! I wish you had the ability to understand how tiring it is to be here, but I doubt *that* will ever happen. I've just got to get back home. On top of everything else, I have a drive to another state ahead of me and I'm so exhausted I don't know if I can make it that far!" Even though I thought having her around somehow eased some of the growing responsibility in dealing with our parents, once my sister left, I realized that she added a significantly stressful component to the mix and I was glad she was gone. I convinced myself that dealing with Mom and Dad's situation by myself was easier than answering to or trying to avoid my sisters.

Before departing, EXHAUSTED TERESA put the finishing touches on a report she and SANCTIMONIOUS SHIRLEY had written. Carefully placed on my parents' kitchen table where I couldn't miss it, the epistle was full of their enumerated observations and instructions; how to sabotage my father's car so he could no longer drive, hiding his keys just in case he figured out what I had done, and calling their various doctors to discuss the number of medications Mom and Dad were taking every day which obviously needed to be pared down. I was to find quality help for them—people who could be trusted. Last, but certainly not least, they created a detailed list of expectations for me, including errand running, grocery shopping, and anything else they could think of that ran on for pages and pages, typed and single spaced.

After reading bits of the sisters' drivel, I decided not to waste any of my time with their trivia. I tore it into dozens of pieces and left it in the trash. The sisters felt relieved by the wisdom of their words. I felt nothing but irritation and loneliness.

∽ ∽ ॐ ∽ ∽

REFLECTION

LISTS

Write things down. Write **everything** down. Make lists... lots of them. If you think that you will remember, I can absolutely confirm that you will not. I say that not to discourage you but to give you a preview of the complexity of managing the life of someone else, as well as your own. The line between the two fades and keeping track of even the most basic activities may become impossible to keep inside your head.

Decide where you will write your lists. If you don't decide, scraps of paper take over your life. You may not notice that life has filled to the overflow, until one fateful moment when you can't find what you need. Failing to retrieve the right scrap of paper containing a bit of vital information, can melt you into a puddle of frustration in the middle of the scraps. Even if it's right in front of you, don't count on being able to see it.

The answer? **Get yourself a snazzy organizer notebook** where you can write everything. It needs to be snazzy so you can find it easily. And it needs to be something that you can grab quickly with one hand. Multi-tasking becomes a familiar way of existence and your list-containing notebook just might save your sanity.

Take a moment. **Get an organizer. Do it NOW!**

CHAPTER 5

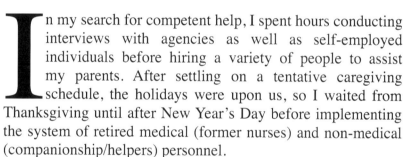

FINDING HELP

In my search for competent help, I spent hours conducting interviews with agencies as well as self-employed individuals before hiring a variety of people to assist my parents. After settling on a tentative caregiving schedule, the holidays were upon us, so I waited from Thanksgiving until after New Year's Day before implementing the system of retired medical (former nurses) and non-medical (companionship/helpers) personnel.

As new people assumed some of my mom's responsibilities, she felt relieved. Although no one approached tasks the way she did, Mom realized how much easier it was for her to have their help. She also enjoyed a side benefit of developing relationships with the staff of caregivers, particularly the college students whom she liked to mother. She learned about their families, what they were studying in school, their hobbies and anything else she could think of. In turn, they doted on her and tried very hard to do things Mom's way.

Dad tolerated the intrusion into their privacy for the sake of my mom and he was glad when each helper's shift was over and the two of them could be alone again.

Most of the time Dad was capable of managing his daily activities by himself. He kept exercising several times each week and continued dealing with their financial affairs, just as he had always done.

A few weeks after the new routine began, Dad decided that I was to be the designated person to take over when he was no longer able. Dad, still well aware of his surroundings, contacted his attorney and asked him to draw up the necessary paperwork. Once the papers were in my dad's possession, he told me of his plan—one that I wasn't at all enthusiastic about. Dad was insistent, and so to pacify him, I eventually agreed, never imagining the implications of his decision.

Within a few weeks of starting the new schedule of helpers for my parents, I realized that I had hired too many caregivers. I made adjustments several times and everything remained fairly constant for a while. We all enjoyed a false sense of security allowing me to believe that everything was under control.

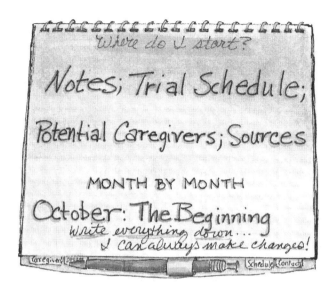

Everything is tentative,

but you have to start somewhere...

REFLECTION

LOOKING

When you don't know how to solve a problem, take a look around. It's surprising how many resources are right in front of you.

Have you ever needed to replace your refrigerator because Old Faithful suddenly gave up the ghost? You look in the ads to see if any store might happen to have a sale on refrigerators because you certainly don't want to pay more than you have to for such an unglamorous, yet necessary item. Good Fortune has smiled on you and multiple stores chose that week to sell refrigerators at a discounted price. How great is that!

What you don't realize is that those same stores frequently sell refrigerators at a reduced price. You never noticed before because you weren't looking.

Life seems to work like that for most anything you need. Give it a try. I bet you'll realize that resources for helping you and the person you care for were there all the time! You didn't need them, so you hadn't noticed before.

Open your eyes and keep looking.

CHAPTER 6

THE HOSPITAL

For the first time in our entire married life, my husband and I lived alone. Our life together spanned more than 30 years and we were, for the first time, without children! My stepdaughter had married and was busy with her own family, while our son's focus remained on designing his life and career.

During those first months after our son left home, my husband and I spent our time getting acquainted with each other, learning to play, and experiencing what it felt like to put each other ahead of everything else in the world. On a whim we could take off for a weekend, enjoy a drive anytime, or talk for hours without interruption. We grew the colorful, wonderful relationship that I had wanted throughout our entire marriage but always had to set aside because of someone else's needs. Exploring new hobbies, working together, and complementing each other's skills, cemented a closeness of which we had only dreamt. Finally, each of us had a soft place to fall and life had become exactly what we wanted it to be—just the two of us.

My husband and I took a vacation in September, the eighth month of my parents' new routine. We drove a few hours to a state lodge where we enjoyed a 3R vacation—rest, relax and refuel. It felt great! Reflecting about our life together, gratitude filled our hearts. Our son's life was on track. My husband's business was doing well. My parents were relatively stable and I was busy building my own lucrative design business and teaching lots of classes. Life felt pretty darn good! As long as it lasted, the illusion of smooth sailing was intoxicating.

Only a couple of weeks after returning from our vacation, my bedroom phone jarred me awake in the pre-dawn hours. With my heart pounding wildly, I listened as the unemotional voice from the emergency monitoring service reported, "Your father, suffering severe chest pains, is being transported to the hospital by ambulance and your mother is remaining in the residence. I have another person listed here—another daughter, I believe. When I hang up with you, I will call and tell her what is happening."

"Thank you," were the only words I could think of. I dropped the phone, looked at my husband and willed myself to move. Dazed and on the verge of panic, my husband and I hurriedly dressed and headed in opposite directions. I raced to my parents' home to my mother, who was alone and surely frightened, while my husband intercepted Dad at the emergency room.

Rushing through the door, I entered my parents' normally orderly living room and noticed the way the couch and chairs had been pushed aside to clear a path for the gurney. A million thoughts streaked through my mind about what those moments must have been like for my dad. I found Mom, still wearing her nightgown, sitting on the bed, staring at the door.

Anxiously I said, "Mom, let's get you dressed."

"Where did they take him? He was so scared..." she said weakly, as tears began to trickle down her cheeks.

"They took Dad to the emergency room so the doctor could help him. What clothes would you like to wear?"

"I don't know... I don't know. Do you think he will be okay?" she asked with growing desperation.

"Mom, the only way I will know that, is if we get to the ER. Let me help you put your clothes on so we can leave," I said, my tone of voice becoming stronger.

"Ok."

Mom felt like a rag doll as I maneuvered her arms and legs into her clothing. It was as if she had no control over her limbs and didn't completely understand what we were doing. After what seemed like an eternity, Mom was ready and I guided her toward their car.

When I arrived at the hospital with Mom, we discovered that Dad was already undergoing tests. Knowing that he had survived a heart attack and cardiac bypass surgery many years before and that his heart had been slowly failing for some time, my ability to remain calm was nearly impossible. After several hours of waiting and diagnostic tests, Dad was admitted to the hospital for further observation. He appeared to be resting with plenty of people to care for him, so I turned my focus back to my mother.

After encouraging my husband to go home, I took my mother to her house to eat and rest. Understandably, she had been quite shaken by the arrival of an ambulance in her driveway and strange people taking her husband away. Mom's behavior seemed odd to me, yet I couldn't put my finger on what I was sensing. I watched her eat a few bites and uncharacteristically push the food away, saying that her stomach was upset. She seemed overtaken by weariness, so I guided her away from the table and tucked her into her bed for a nap. Even in her somewhat confused state, Mom insisted that I go home.

Driving across town, I found my husband waiting for me at home.

He greeted me at the door and asked, "What can I do to help?"

"Nothing. I just have to wait and see what happens," I responded. "Something about Mom is really strange. I know she was terribly upset by everything that happened with Dad, but she just isn't herself at all."

After a moment he said softly, "I'll do whatever you need me to do."

"I know," I said.

Pulling me into his chest with his strong arms, I knew that together we could handle whatever might happen.

Only an hour after I left Mom, she called. When I answered my phone, I heard an almost inaudible voice say, "I think you'd better come back here right away."

"Mom? What's going on?"

"I don't know. I feel... I feel sick."

I found Mom sitting at the kitchen table staring into space with an assortment of my dad's belongings in her lap; her abnormal demeanor puzzled me. We packed the odd things that Mom wanted to take to my dad and climbed back into the car. En route to the hospital, I told Mom that I thought we should stop by the emergency room before visiting my dad. I knew that an elderly person, once dehydrated, could quickly become disoriented. Mom was so frail that I was afraid even a minor bout of nausea could be the cause of her problem. I hoped that some fluids and medical attention might resolve the issue. She was mildly resistant, but cooperative as I explained my concern. After arriving at the hospital and getting Mom settled with someone to care for her in the ER, I was given a stack of papers for the second time in only a few hours. As quickly as my shaky hand would write, I entered Mom's information in the familiar blanks. Turning to a nurse I said, "I'll be back. I need to check on my dad."

As I arrived on the floor where I left him, I was intercepted by a nurse.

"Your father has been moved to another unit for closer observation," she stated.

Fighting the urge to be sick, I managed to ask the nurse, "Where is he?"

"MICU, third floor, ma'am," the nurse said pointing toward the elevator.

My heart skipped a beat as I heard an explosion of words in my head. "Oh God, what is going on?"

I spent the remainder of that twilight-zone day traveling on an elevator from Dad on the third floor to Mom in the emergency room, trying to comfort them, each fraught with concern for the other. I didn't know whom to worry about the most as I felt myself stretching thinner and thinner. Dad's condition worsened and he was not responding to the chosen medications. At the same time, no definitive diagnosis seemed obvious for my mother and she was not improving. In every opportunity with nurses and doctors, I pleaded that Mom be admitted for additional evaluation. Trying to be on two different floors was difficult, but having one of them in the hospital and the other at home was impossible.

I was approaching a breaking point with none of my sisters in sight. With Dad's medical history and knowing that the emergency monitoring service had also phoned EXHAUSTED TERESA early that morning, I was sure that my sisters were en route to the hospital and would be arriving at any moment.

Instead, in the late afternoon, their phone calls began.

My sisters wanted answers from me. I was supposed to tell each of them whether or not to come *home*. Their questions circled my head like a swarm of bees. "How serious is Dad?" "What is wrong with Mother?" "How long will they be in the hospital?" "Do you *really* think we need to be there?"

How could I know what to tell my sisters? It was too soon to have much information about anything. Navigating the emergency room twice in one day, dealing with more nurses and doctors than I could count and trying to be in multiple locations at once left me completely dazed. My physical stamina disappeared, and in its place remained only spinning thoughts. "Could Dad possibly survive this? What am I going to tell Mom? What is wrong with her? What if something terrible is wrong with both of them? How long could this possibly last? What do I do next? Where is my family? Why aren't they here? How could they leave me alone to make all these decisions?" On and on the questions spun...

Saturday ended with Mom, given a generic diagnosis of complications from diabetes, staying on one floor while Dad rested in the Medical Intensive Care Unit. I went home, seeking reserves for the unknown journey looming ahead, hoping that my husband was keeping a place called **normal**, somewhere.

REFLECTION

INSANITY

The dictionary housed within my computer defines insanity as the **state of being seriously mentally ill; madness.**

You might find that definition oddly encouraging. You're able to get up, get dressed, go about the day, and manage to take care of what you must. Everything feels so unfamiliar—as though you stepped into another dimension. The state that you might label **insanity** is really disorientation. You have somehow lost the stake that you always used to nail down reality. That's why it feels like the ground is shifting under your feet.

You think, "This must be what it feels like to be crazy!"

Relax for a moment and know that you are not going mad! Disoriented, yes. Insane, absolutely not. Life may have heaved a bomb your direction, leading you to believe that everything you knew to be true has disappeared into smoke. Just realize that even though the ground is shifting beneath you, it's still there. Why not take off your shoes, wiggle your toes and feel the earth. It may feel like standing in sand as the waves sweep in and out around your feet. In spite of your physical size, the ocean erodes the sand right out from under you. If the waves crash hard enough, you might even fall down. Oddly enough, even if you fall, there is still ground under you. Don't worry about the shape. It will continue to change and it may be different tomorrow than it is today.

You are okay and you're definitely not going crazy.

CHAPTER 7

SLEEP

rom the moment my phone rang on Saturday morning, my ability to sleep proportionately diminished with each decision I made about my parents. I'd heard other people describe the disruption of sleep as **hospital-head** or **caregiver's syndrome**. In a sort of oddly comforting way, I appreciated the affirmation that I wasn't the only person who had experienced this shift. Never before in my life had sleep been so elusive.

Several days after my parents' admission to the hospital, my body, no longer able to function, kindly collapsed. Sleep briefly took me away from the reality of the hospital, and from talking, thinking, planning, and fearing the unknown. The blessed break didn't last very long; just long enough to keep me going.

As time marched on I discovered that when I did sleep, I visited a marvelous place where my spirit sometimes quieted enough to receive a bit of clarity. I lost track of the times when I felt as though I were drowning in the ocean of decisions, having no idea what step to take next. Without explanation, in the place between sleep and awakening, reliable answers often bubbled up and upon fully waking, I trusted the guidance.

The stress of caring for my parents never again lessened as, during any twenty-four hour period, there was always more to deal with than humanly possible. Hours turned into days. Days became weeks. Weeks grew into months and months eventually became years. My sleep difficulties continued and ironically, when I finally found the time to sleep, somehow, I seemed to have forgotten how.

REFLECTION

REST VS. SLEEP

You might think that rest and sleep are interchangeable words for the same activity. Go without sleep and your body begins to betray you by systems shutting down and erratic thinking. Your body needs sleep to repair itself and to reset for the next awake-period. Not sleeping is a lot like not eating or drinking. Stop eating, drinking or sleeping and you can't sustain yourself very long. Sometimes during a time of unusual stress, you may find the ability to sleep nearly impossible. The mind/body doesn't wind down far enough to let you drift off. So, what can you do if sleep won't visit you? First of all, don't worry about going to sleep. Worrying about **not** sleeping only makes it harder to fall asleep.

Try taking a **rest**.

Rest does not have to involve sleep but it does require you to stop your activity. Resting allows you to somewhat refresh, relax and recover. Sit for a while and put up your feet. Watch a pointless movie or read a romance novel or a magazine.

Better yet, treat yourself to some sort of electronic device that, along with a set of headphones, allows you to enter another world through guided meditation, music, or listening to an audio book. And while you're at it, during these mini-respite breaks, enjoy the side benefit of blocking out noises like the phone and droning conversations.

One other thing—know that eventually sleep will return to you. It might not be the same as before the period of stress, but you will sleep again.

For the time being, just take a rest.

What is without periods of rest

will not endure

– Ovid

CHAPTER 8

BROKEN HEARTS

Sunday morning, 24 hours after my dad entered the hospital, I was summoned by his doctors. Upon arriving I was told that Dad had suffered a heart attack. As if that weren't enough for Dad's body to deal with, the intravenous blood-thinning drugs were causing major problems. Nonstop, frightening nose bleeds were just one of the visible side effects.

Recognizing the fear I was attempting to conceal, one of the doctors asked to speak to me. "The dilemma that we're facing is significant. Your father is now bleeding internally as well as externally—a side effect of the medication we're using. It's the best choice that we have, given your father's heart condition. But now, it's difficult to say whether it's helping or hurting him. If we discontinue the drug, he may experience blood clots. If one of those gets to his lung…" His voice trailed off as he seemed to be thinking about what next to say to me.

"If this were your father, what would you do?" I asked.

"That's really difficult for me to say. We do need you to make a decision about discontinuing the medication. Things are not likely to get better," he stated.

Evaluating the risk fell in my lap. Dad was understandably overwhelmed by his physical problems and fear. Mom was too weak and confused to comprehend as I tried to explain my conversation with the doctor. Dad was experiencing so many problems that I had little time to think. I had to immediately make a decision—one that felt like my own chest was being crushed. Discontinuing the drugs was my choice. Managing his pain and keeping my dad comfortable became the plan.

There was no new procedure or medication that would fix his heart, or mine.

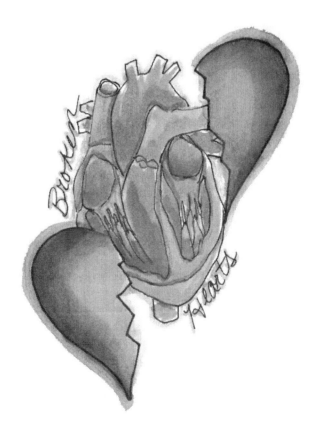

Mom experienced disorientation and a great deal of anxiety in the hospital. She was fearful that something had happened to my dad and I had not told her. Mom always appeared to be so fragile that I didn't know how much information to give her. During their 65 year marriage, my dad had always been their decision maker and Mom's protector. As she and I continued along our path, I discovered that not knowing the truth was much worse for her than dealing with difficult situations head on. With time and patience I began to more fully recognize and understand aspects of my mother's personality that I had never seen which eventually led us into a much deeper, more loving relationship.

Riding the hospital elevator and making difficult decisions filled another day as I checked on my parents and tried to find doctors. Wherever I was, I should have been somewhere else. I needed some magic, a clone or even a sibling to share the load.

The human heart feels things that eyes cannot see, and knows what the mind cannot understand.

– Robert Valett

REFLECTION

MAKING DECISIONS

S ome people seem to make decisions with ease and confidence. It may even appear that they don't have to invest much thought in the process before deciding. Others agonize over the tiniest detail and procrastinate as they torture themselves with possible outcomes.

Do you see yourself as one of these decision makers or are you somewhere in the middle? During my own caregiving journey, I tended to be the agonizer—trying to figure out all the ramifications of a decision before actually making it. As time passed and decisions stacked up, I grew to be more comfortable with the process and outcomes.

When you assume the role of caregiver, you will encounter numerous decisions you must make. Some decisions carry little consequence while others may be life altering. How will you ever make the **right** decision? If you have the luxury of time, gather information and make the best choice that you can with the information that you have. If time is short you may have to make a decision and hope for the best.

Decision making is rarely easy, but it comes with the caregiving territory. Humans are not omniscient, so none of us can know all the possible outcomes resulting from our decisions. Someone once told me, "A decision made at a given time is the right one for that moment." Read those words again and if you have difficulty remembering them, write them on sticky notes and plaster them around yourself.

Go ahead and make the decision. Rest in knowing that it's the right one for now.

CHAPTER 9

THE FILE CABINET

I left the hospital briefly, because I realized that I needed to locate the paperwork my parents created the previous summer. Entering my parents' home, I was greeted by their two lonely cats who nearly tripped me as they wound through my legs. I walked into my dad's office and for the first time in my life, approached his off-limits file cabinet. It was Dad's private space where no one, not even Mom, would venture. Thumbing through files, I thought about the way my dad overpowered me with his decision that I, alone, was to have legal responsibility for them, regardless of my hesitance. When Dad made a decision of such importance, his unspoken rule of compliance became effective and I was clearly not allowed to refuse. As a sigh of surrender left my body, I kept looking.

Continuing my hunt for the papers, I wondered why the file cabinet was off limits. Dad never verbally said so. It just was. Many months later, when I had time, I discovered that Dad's file cabinet housed valuable parts of his life, along with reams of unnecessary papers kept for reasons known only to him. I found countless written prayers and copies of sermons from church services, receipts for every car he purchased and carbon copies of dozens of letters he had written, randomly mixed among files containing legal and vital papers.

Gratitude overwhelmed me when I discovered several carefully constructed folders containing documents with Mom and Dad's wishes along with the power of attorney that proved I had authority to be their advocate and make decisions on their behalf. Tucked in beside the paperwork I was relieved to find the checkbook to which we had added my imprinted name and signature. I stuck the checkbook in the folder of paperwork and wondered what else I might need.

I glanced in the bedroom and noticed Dad's wallet on the dresser. Something beckoned me to open it and there I found Mom and Dad's insurance and Medicare cards. Beside his dollar bills I noticed the car wash coupons that I had given him for his ninetieth birthday, just days before he entered the hospital. Sifting through random notes in Dad's wallet, I wondered if we had celebrated his last birthday. Tears suddenly welled up. But this was not the time to cry or sit with my head in my hands, even though the little girl inside me begged to do so. She had to wait as details at the hospital demanded my attention.

REFLECTION

PAPERS

P apers are a necessity, but they can take over your life. Papers can be neatly filed or just stacked up until they spill into chaos. Depending on the writer, papers may carry condemnation or permission.

Certain papers are essential for a caregiver. Financial and health care powers of attorney fall into this category. Without them, your ability to advocate on behalf of someone is quite limited. Also, be sure that you know where those papers are located, who created them and how much power they give you. You might consider seeking a second opinion regarding the strength of the paperwork. You can never have too much information regarding protection of your family member or yourself. The original papers need to be kept in a safe place and copies carried with you in your snazzy organizer.

If your family member has a trust or will (or both), you need to know the location of the original documents and have copies in your organizer. Dealing with government agencies, insurance companies and financial advisers often requires that you have copies of certain pages.

In addition to keeping track of legal papers, lots of other paperwork will arrive in the mail. If you can stay organized, you may feel less pressure as time goes by. And if you can't deal with the onslaught of papers, put them somewhere so you can eventually deal with them.

Sometimes, the paperwork has to wait.

I have so much paperwork, I'm afraid

my paperwork has paperwork.

– Gabrielle Zerin

CHAPTER 10

SECOND FLOOR

My parents' stay in the hospital stretched into the fourth day. By Tuesday, the nurses and doctors decided that Dad had stabilized enough to be moved out of the Medical Intensive Care Unit. The staff located a room where Mom and Dad could be together in adjoining beds. Once Mom could see my dad and hold his hand, she relaxed. Her disorientation (commonly called Sundowners Syndrome) continued at night but daylight usually brought her back to reality.

I learned to travel with all legal paperwork and a notebook in an aqua colored plastic envelope, my constant companion. It housed the expanding accumulation of papers and notes from conversations with the social worker, doctors and the care-coordinator nurse, the most valuable resource of all. That special nurse kept tabs on everything happening in the second floor room where my parents rested. Rarely had she seen an elderly couple in the hospital as patients at the same time and her genuine concern was reassuring. As my parents' uncertain condition confused me, the care-coordinator explained terminology and calmed my growing fear.

By Wednesday, *EXHAUSTED TERESA* and *WEAK WANDA* (my sister who played dumb and incapable in order to escape any family responsibility) arrived. The shock of seeing our parents forced them from their imaginary worlds where everything would be okay and Mom and Dad would live happily ever after. I had been coping with so many extraordinary events that I never really noticed the state of my sisters. As soon as I dealt with one issue concerning Mom or Dad, another arose and my energy to care for my sisters or what they were feeling simply didn't exist.

Late that afternoon, Dad experienced another cardiac event. All his doctors converged for a conference. Their conclusion was succinctly explained by the cardiologist. "There is nothing else that we can do. We have exhausted our options. Your father may last a few days or a few weeks." He was aloof and unemotional as he delivered the truth, and that helped me discover a stoic self control I needed in that moment and in the succeeding days… weeks…months…

More relatives arrived Wednesday night because my two sisters sounded the panic-alarm due to Dad's cardiac episode. *SANCTIMONIOUS SHIRLEY* was not among them.

After their tiring visits, most of the extra people left as there was little anyone could do to help. For some reason, that night *EXHAUSTED TERESA* and *WEAK WANDA* decided that they distrusted the hospital staff to care for our parents. The two of them fashioned beds out of chairs, and stayed in the room with Mom and Dad through through the night. *WEAK WANDA,* although camouflaged by her self-created inadequacy, loved our parents from some distant internal space. Of all of us, she was undoubtedly the most visibly shaken by the thought of losing our parents. *EXHAUSTED TERESA* found *WEAK WANDA'S* energy contagious and so the two of them stuck together, bonded by some invisible familial glue. I felt the need to conserve my energy for whatever happened next, so I refused to share the night shift. My decision was not well received by my sisters, but the hospital staff seemed grateful to have one less person in the room… And so the vigil continued.

REFLECTION

SELF-CONTROL

How do you control yourself in an uncontrollable situation? Isn't that a great question? How I wish there were a simple answer, but here is one way to look at it. If the situation with which you are dealing is out of your control, the only thing you can control, is your **self**. You can dissolve into a million emotional pieces or you can choose to deal with whatever is in front of you.

Falling apart may be exactly what you want to do for lots of justifiable reasons. Maybe you are too young to deal with what's happening. Maybe you find yourself alone with no support. Maybe the choices that you are facing are life altering, for you or for someone else. Life doesn't always seem fair and now is a good time for some acceptance.

It's time to reach deep and find your **self**. It's there. Your **self** is the part of you that you can trust. It's the part that speaks to you when you desperately need an answer. Now is the time for your self to show up to help you deal—right now!

Decide to fall apart later. There will be plenty of time after the crisis. Make a date with yourself to disintegrate when you can do it in style. You will deserve it!

For now you need to control that which you can—your self.

Not being able to govern events,

I govern myself.

– Michel de Montaigne

CHAPTER 11

NO CHANGE

Very little changed on Thursday. Like the preceding string of days, time had no measurement. I waited and watched. I hoped and prayed for something—anything that might make the situation better. I continued talking with medical personnel and monitored Dad's condition throughout the day. Time dragged on. Dad seemed to be somewhat stable and was aware of his surroundings most of the time. Mom, although weak and disoriented throughout the night, continued making progress. No longer swathed in confusion, she usually recognized me, and her appetite seemed to be returning.

Late in the day I stayed with Mom and Dad while my vigilant sisters took a break. As Dad slept in the adjacent bed, I crawled in with Mom, laid beside her, and held her thin, fragile hand. We watched a funny television show that made us both laugh. I didn't know who was comforting whom, but we both felt safe, even if it was only for a few moments. In actuality I wasn't really watching the television. I was pretending to be a little girl whose mommy would make sure everything was okay. Mom always assumed the position of worrier so I didn't have to, but in a flash when the phone rang with the news of my dad and the ambulance, the roles reversed and I took over the job. The idea of being in a hospital room with both of my parents was never, ever the tiniest possibility in my mind. Yet, there we were—the three of us with all the responsibility congesting my heart. Surviving those days, filled with uncertainty, I functioned using instinct and logic, because I didn't dare actually feel what was happening.

Friday arrived and I learned from my sisters that the previous night was as incoherent as all the others for Mom and Dad. Their lack of routine and loss of familiarity had taken its toll on each of them.

In spite of the uncertainty of our parents' future, each player in the cast of characters I called family, enacted their roles perfectly. WEAK WANDA, after spending 48 tiring hours with Mom and Dad returned to her home because "she had her own life to live." Long ago she had been a compassionate, loving daughter, but over time she evolved into a self-absorbed existence where little else mattered. Although WEAK WANDA lived less than a half-day's drive away, due to her "very busy life," she managed to keep her visits with Mom and Dad to once or twice a year. Her interaction with our parents amounted to a weekly phone call and apparently, that was enough to soothe her conscience. SANCTIMONIOUS SHIRLEY'S decision not to make the trip to be with Mom and Dad in the hospital, was predictable. If God didn't tell her to do it, she didn't, and apparently her request about spending time with our parents was met with silence. EXHAUSTED TERESA, overtaken by her stress level and anxious to go home, remained and watched me to see what I planned to do about Mom and Dad.

As the care-coordinator, social worker, and I conferenced, I tried to be sensible and unemotional in order to make the best choices for my parents. The decision about follow-up care vacillated from sending them to a skilled nursing facility, or to a nursing home, or back to their own home with additional care. Each choice was like an iceberg. What little I could actually see was supported by the vast unknown that lay below the surface.

Every decision was left to me as my sisters silently waited and watched, seldom lending encouragement or support.

I felt the invisible weight on my shoulders growing with each passing moment. Where would I find the wisdom and common sense to make a decision that impacted all of us? Trying to contemplate the decision, my mind chose instead to wander through a cocoon of memories. I remembered my dad's strength and determination as he added on to our home in 117° summer heat to create a nicer house for his growing family.

In my mind, I wandered through my dad's beautiful flower and vegetable gardens. I remembered Mom and Dad telling me the stories about their years of canning meat and vegetables throughout the night and into the early morning hours in order to feed our large family. I relived the books Mom read to me at bedtime and remembered how she listened to me rattle on every day after school as she prepared our evening meal.

While in high school and college, Mom and Dad supported my interests and activities rarely missing a musical performance, play, or basketball game. As my mind skipped from one memory to another, the hurt and rejection I'd felt from Mom and Dad so many years ago, melted away.

In those moments I accepted that they were human just like me and capable of making a much regretted choice. Accepting their humanity allowed me, also, to accept my own. In that moment, my memories filled me with warmth and seemed to magically erase the emptiness created at the time of my wedding. In place of the void I found a well of courage—something I needed to draw from frequently as our life together unfolded.

Reluctantly, I crawled out of my memory-cocoon to find reality waiting. In spite of trying not to... I remembered. A decision must be made.

REFLECTION

MEMORIES

The mind is a busy thing! It thinks and processes information, all while recording ongoing events.

For a few minutes, take a look back into those mindful recordings and notice what you see as you skip from one picture to another. Some may be disconcerting, others hurtful, but I bet you will see some happy events unfold, too.

Do you remember watching a child discover something? Have you ever walked with a dog and observed its joy in every detail? What about sitting in your mom's lap? Christmas morning chaos? Do you remember listening to someone read you a story? Going to camp? Learning a new skill? What about your first paycheck?

The point is that our minds are constantly recording. Select a couple of the happiest memories to think about when you find yourself engulfed by stress and difficult decision making. Going back to your chosen memory can take you on a brief vacation from the moment, bringing a smile to your heart. Take advantage of every break you can create, even if you only find it inside your own memory bank.

One other thing... Remember, even in the midst of all the current stress, you can record the good memories as you participate in them.

A good memory could be the very thing that sustains you.

CHAPTER 12

ANXIETY AND ARRANGEMENTS

Monday morning began with a phone call from *Exhausted Teresa*, reporting that Mom was having additional problems. As I drove to the hospital, my irritation quickly escalated into anger that my sister could not handle the situation. Clearly, she expected me to do something to make everything better. As the baby of the family, my sisters didn't particularly respect me, so trying to understand their dependence on me was strange and infuriating.

When I arrived, through her confusion Mom somehow managed to communicate to me that she was tired and very uncomfortable. After more blood tests and discussions with the care-coordinator, we suspected Mom's lack of mobility from being in bed so many days had slowed the metabolization of a specific medication, causing her increased discomfort and grogginess.

Once again, we waited to see what would happen and hoped that time might ease Mom's situation. I watched Dad worry about Mom and when Mom was aware, she was very worried about Dad. Neither of them had any concept about the gravity of their circumstances.

The time to make the decision had arrived. I needed to make arrangements because my parents, according to their doctors, were to be released from the hospital the following day. The doctors concluded that, in spite of appearances, Mom was progressing well. Wherever Mom went, Dad would go, too. Their destination was my dilemma. With only 24 hours left, I had a lot of choices and preparations to make.

With my husband's help and support, we spent the remainder of Monday arranging a care plan I thought might work and buying medical equipment as well as creating an organizer to house care notes, medications, and phone calls. We installed a message board where I could leave notes for the staff of new people I had employed, ordered oxygen, and added grab bars and other bathroom necessities.

I had no idea if we had covered all the bases, but knowing that my husband could remodel or repair just about anything helped ease my anxiety. Never once did he refuse to stop what he was doing when I needed his assistance. When I thought of something that might make life easier for my parents, my husband was the first and only person, to make it happen.

When everything was arranged to the best of my ability, I went back to the hospital and crawled up on Mom's bed, took her hand in mine, and said, "Tomorrow is going to be a big day! It's time to go home."

The response is one I will always remember.

In unison my parents asked, "Really? Are you sure?"

"Yes, really!" I responded. "I'm springing you from this joint tomorrow!"

The spontaneous looks of relief on their faces temporarily dissolved my feelings of uncertainty. I decided that coping with the moment rather than imagining problems would be our new plan.

And so we began the next adventure.

꒰ ꒰ ꒰ ꒰ ꒰

Life belongs to the living and he who lives

must be prepared for changes.

– Goethe

REFLECTION

EQUIPMENT

There is a steep learning curve for a new caregiver. Rarely does one plan or aspire to be a family caregiver. You might know in the back of your mind that caregiving is a possibility someday, but you stow it away in the "maybe-but-I-sure-hope-not" file.

An emergency occurs or a slow decline brings awareness that changes must be made. With either option usually comes an accumulation of equipment. Locating and acquiring what you need is exhausting, even daunting, until you realize that without the invention of these amazing aids, life would be much more taxing for everyone. The end result is often greater independence for the person that you care for, translating into less dependence on you.

Entire stores and websites specialize in mobility, as well as medical aids and equipment. Sometimes people are resistant to the idea of accepting help. Regardless of an obstinate attitude, keep looking at the possibilities. Never assume that you know everything or that your situation cannot be improved. Ingenious people are constantly designing new items and when you discover one, give it consideration. If someone offers to give you things that they no longer need, take them. That's one more thing you don't have to buy. If you acquire a duplicate, consider carrying it in your car, or pass it along to someone else in need.

When you find yourself overwhelmed by the enormity of your situation, stop for a moment in gratitude for all the things available to help you. Without them, I can tell you, life would be much harder.

CHAPTER 13

MY FEAR

Late in the afternoon, after all the stress surrounding the hospital ordeal and making preparations for Mom and Dad to return to their home, I stopped for a much needed break with my husband. As we enjoyed being together, looking into each other's tired eyes and sipping a cup of coffee, a tidal wave of emotion suddenly swept over me. My husband patiently waited for my tears to subside and listened as I rambled on trying to find some perspective by describing my overwhelming fear with words.

"What will happen when I take my parents home? Will anyone in my family help me since they all live in other towns and are so conveniently busy when I need them? Do I really have the capacity to care for my parents? Can I actually manage a staff of people? Where will the money come from? Have I made the best decision to take them back home?"

My imagination was frantic as one fearful question chased another.

And then the most haunting question of all; "What if I take Mom and Dad home where they sit in their chairs and draw their last breaths?" More tears streamed down my cheeks as I forced myself to consider a possibility that I had been avoiding. After a few silent moments, clarity floated to the surface.

"Where else would my parents want to take that last breaths? A nursing home? The hospital?"

I possessed no ability to see into the future, so I just had to choose an option and see what happened. Holding my husband's hand, my fear gradually subsided. I realized and welcomed the knowledge that I was giving Mom and Dad the gift of home and familiarity and freedom to be where they most wanted to be.

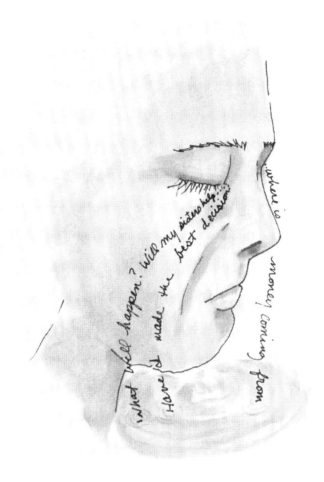

Courage is resistance to fear,

mastery of fear—not absence of fear.

– Mark Twain

REFLECTION

FACING FEAR

Have you ever felt so much fear that you don't even know what you are afraid of? Fear can immobilize you or propel you into a state of hyperactivity. Either reaction interferes with you living your own life.

Being so fearful that you cannot move steals your experiences as well as your joy. You become caught in a noose that constricts tighter and tighter as you feel fear growing to the point of suffocation or paralysis.

The opposite fear-state of hyperactivity keeps you so busy that you can't think of anything except the 10 things you have to do in the next 2 hours because the world will cave in if you don't. The consequences of not accomplishing the tasks are so fear-filled, that you drive faster, eat faster, sleep less, talk quicker and multi-task, continually.

Going back to the original question… stop for a moment and ask, "What am I afraid of?" Face the fear squarely. Don't look away. Give yourself permission to listen to the fear. Give yourself permission to look at it. What shape is the fear? What does the fear sound like? What does it feel like?

If you can answer those questions, then just notice what happens to it. Your acknowledgment is the power over the fear.

One last thing about fear... the antidote to fear is gratitude. It's very difficult to be fearful and grateful at the same time. So, be grateful and watch your fears begin to melt away.

Life is a gift, not to be wasted in fear.

CHAPTER 14

HOMECOMING

Tuesday morning finally arrived. Mom and Dad were wheeled out in chairs to their waiting van. We made our trek home loaded with flowers, personal items and all of the accumulated paraphernalia from their ten-day hospital stay. While my parents were in the hospital tethered to IVs and oxygen tubes, the trees had changed into their autumn attire. Listening to Mom and Dad's conversation as I drove them home was amusing. It was as if they had never before seen the beautiful colors of the maples and oaks.

Two very lonesome cats and one of the hired caregivers, a retired nurse, celebrated our arrival. With great effort and assistance from newly acquired walkers, Mom and Dad labored up the ramp into their home to their respective recliners. I watched as they sat with smiles of gratitude and laps full of felines. I had never seen two happier people!

EXHAUSTED TERESA managed to partially unload some of Mom and Dad's belongings from her car before collapsing in a chair beside our parents. She expected someone else to finish the job of emptying her vehicle because she had to rest before leaving to go back to her own home. All of us were relieved when she finally packed her suitcase and left a couple of hours later. Just being in the presence of someone who projected such tired energy made everyone feel as though their feet were too heavy to lift.

After lunch and settling my parents in bed for naps, I intended to spend the afternoon shopping for groceries, filling new prescriptions and preparing supper. I couldn't think of a better way to celebrate Mom and Dad's homecoming than with our family's favorite meal—roast beef and Dutch dumplings. It was the best comfort food because it smelled good and tasted even better.

With the shopping completed, I returned to their home, unloaded everything and found Dad out of bed, back in his recliner, experiencing chest pains. I tried to remain calm in spite of my rapidly increasing anxiety. "Dad, where are your emergency heart pills located?"

He replied, "I tried to find some, but I don't think I have any." My illusion of being prepared instantly disappeared. With my panic growing by the second, I called the care-coordinator at the hospital. She instructed me about applying one of Dad's nitro patches as a temporary measure while she ordered more pills, requiring another trip to the pharmacy. Finally, after what seemed like hours, Dad's chest pain subsided and we both began breathing normally.

I finished preparing their meal and, with overwhelming gratitude as the first day at home came to a close, we ate. With hugs and a few tears, I left Mom and Dad in the care of their new overnight caregiver, and drove to my own home, completely fatigued.

Home, the spot of earth supremely blest,

A dearer, sweeter spot than all the rest.

– Robert Montgomery

REFLECTION

PHARMACY

One great frustration you may encounter while caregiving is understanding medications. Unless you have a medical background, visits to the pharmacy and learning strange words while working out dosing schedules, possible side effects and more, can be extremely overwhelming. Here are my recommendations:

First, keep an up-to-date master list of all medications, noting the purpose of each drug. If the person you care for is taking multiple drugs, this list will relieve you from remembering countless details and repeatedly reading prescription bottles. On your list, include the drug name, dosage, number of doses per day and time of day to be given. It's even helpful to make note of the color and shape of the pill. Also, note whether the drug is to be given with or without food and any dietary restrictions. Take an updated medication list to every medical appointment and keep a copy in your organizer for quick reference in case of an emergency. If any medication adjustment is ordered, be sure to update your master list.

Secondly, purchase a medication organizer from your pharmacy so that you or the person managing the medications can set up the drugs on a weekly basis. Establish a system for ordering refills one day per week. By staying organized, you will be less likely to run out of a given drug, keeping confusion to a minimum.

Thirdly, if possible choose an independent pharmacy and become personally acquainted with the pharmacist. This invaluable person can educate you, keep you apprised of possible drug interactions, side effects to watch for, generic substitutes and available rebates. If you must use a large chain pharmacy, make it a point to establish a relationship with one or two of the pharmacists. Learn their names and find out when they work.

And lastly, be sure to ask questions. Understanding medication management can be tricky. Never let embarrassement stop you.

Do anything possible to make your job easier.

CHAPTER 15

THE FOG

After only a couple of weeks of the new schedule, I didn't know where I was. Trips to Mom and Dad's were so frequent that I lost count. My car seemed to drive itself from my house across town to my parents'. Although the care plan included a morning caregiving shift and one person to stay each night, there was no one to cover the afternoon/early evening hours. Trying to conserve as much money as possible, I filled the open shifts. In addition, I needed to orient all the new caregivers so each one understood how to help my parents.

Mom and Dad, both extremely weak after all the days in the hospital, recognized little of what I was doing and, in a way, their ignorance was a blessing. In another way, I hopelessly wanted them to help me. Repeatedly I had conversations with my helpers about the possibility of either of my parents dying at home. I heard myself saying words in some odd, clinically removed manner as I seemed to develop a sort of split persona, enabling one part of me to talk without emotion. When getting in my car to go home, the other person—the child within—crawled into my lap, sobbing for her mommy to come back and take care of her.

I never imagined that being a grown-up would be this hard.

Not even one month had gone by since the hospital ordeal. It was still October, but I felt like I had been doing this for months or years. I was almost sure that I was living some other October. It certainly couldn't be the same October, could it? Every day challenged me. I was running two households and trying to remember who had onions. It seemed that I was always buying onions and putting them in the wrong refrigerator. I spent an unbelievable quantity of time in grocery stores and pharmacies. More often than not, getting a prescription filled required two trips because of the frustrating partnership between pharmacies and insurance companies.

I struggled to stay organized to keep everything going.

The silence between my thoughts no longer existed. Constant whirling questions, as I second-guessed my decisions, drowned out the pleadings from my own soul for help. I ping-ponged from the incessant chatter of my thoughts back to a familiar mind-numbing fog. Back and forth... in and out... around and back.... questions... chatter... fog...

Not even one month had gone by...

REFLECTION

BEING A GROWN-UP

As a little girl, I always loved the story of *Peter Pan*. And to this day I still love the part about not growing up.

The day I fully realized I was a grown-up proved an eye-opening day and one I didn't embrace very easily. It happened when I became the parent, and my parents became the children. I didn't realize what had happened for a while and when I did, I desperately wanted our roles to reverse. I couldn't imagine where I would find the wisdom I needed to parent my parents.

The irony is that as a child, I couldn't wait to be a grown-up. Everyone was older than I was and I thought they had coveted privileges. I blinked, and one day I was all grown up. I thought I must have been the only one, because so many people looked to me for answers.

Being grown up was very scary at times and definitely wasn't my choice. It was, however, my reality. I had to be responsible. I had to go places whether I wanted to or not. Sometimes, I had to make very difficult decisions. And sometimes my decisions impacted my life and the lives of my parents in unanticipated ways.

Little by little, I realized that being a grown-up wasn't so bad. Acceptance replaced anxiety. I discovered a new relationship with my parents and I realized that my attitude was far more important than my decision making.

Grown-ups have perspective that children don't. Grown-ups understand that life is too short to waste and too long to be miserable.

CHAPTER 16

MONEY

As one problem resolved, another arrived, but dealing with money was constant. My dad had always handled their financial matters. Mom contentedly let him deal with all monetary issues over the years, but now he was no longer capable as his interest in money amounted to counting the loose change in his desk. Taking possession of his checkbook elicited an uneasiness within me as though I had intruded into his private domain, but my parents wanted to stay in their own home and that required money to pay the hired caregivers who made Mom and Dad's desire reality.

Initially, I had very little information to work with, including details of monthly income from Dad's retirement, social security, or investments. Searching and asking questions became second nature to me. I knew that my dad had invested money, and I remembered a notebook he had shown me several times containing his financial information. I later realized that Dad's notebook was not a completely accurate picture, although he had been adamant about its scope. There were many surprises—a few of them pleasant. When moving his investments from one place to another, Dad sometimes forgot to record the change in his private notebook. My discoveries always had a way of showing up just when we needed them most.

Accepting each day as a new opportunity, I paid every bill, purchased groceries and kept supplies on hand for whatever situation arose. I did whatever had to be done and somehow, there was enough money. When the hospital and doctor bills began arriving, I had no idea how that was going to work out as I knew little about Medicare and insurance. The plastic envelope, my constant companion, grew thicker and thicker with information, essential cards, and stuff I was afraid to discard. There were papers to file and questions to answer requiring information that, surprisingly enough, I could retrieve—usually from my trusty envelope. I functioned on a fast, undeniable learning curve as each day presented a fresh opportunity to practice trust.

Looking back, I wonder when I stumbled into that place of surrender and trust. I am an intelligent woman, but I am far from knowing answers to questions that I never thought to ask. As weariness replaced clear thinking, the principle of self-preservation emerged from somewhere. I was forced to let go and trust something far greater than myself to direct my actions. With my heart in the right place, mistakes could be made and overcome. But, I realized that I still had to take action. I could not sit back and wait for instructions to be delivered to me on a silver platter. "Do what is in front of your face" became my guiding principle during a very dimly lit time.

The rest of my family seemed quite content to sit back and silently observe from afar. Although Dad was no longer able to deal with financial matters, he could still make his opinion very clear to everyone. My sisters never, ever considered questioning our father about his choices. And, my dad apparently never felt the need to explain his decision to place the burden of responsibility solely on my shoulders. As time passed, I wished many times that he had, **just once**, explained to everyone why he chose me to carry on in his place.

As I cared for my parents, money proved not only a challenge but one of my most powerful teachers. The only way to describe that period of time—**Trust**. I trusted that if I asked a question, an answer would arrive. I trusted that if I needed more help, I would find it. I trusted that when I needed money, it would show up from somewhere. I learned that trust plus surrender equaled survival.

∽ ∽ ❦ ∽ ∽

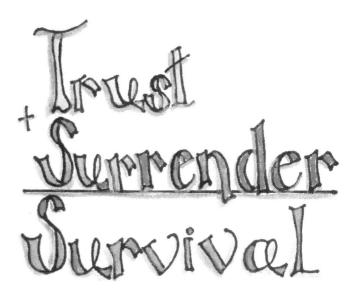

REFLECTION

FINANCES

Money is energy. Believe it or not! It ebbs and flows. Sometimes there is just not enough and sometimes without explanation, there is abundance.

Is there a secret you should know about money? Actually, there are two secrets.

- **First, be grateful**. Be grateful for everything related to finances. Make a list of what you are grateful for—every bill that gets paid—every necessity you can purchase—every extra dollar that shows up. And, be grateful for the discovery of programs and agencies that are available to help extend your finances.

- **Second, Ask & Trust**. The second secret you should know is two-fold. First, ask. Secondly, trust.

Never be afraid to ask questions about finances. There are lots of resources available waiting to provide answers. Keep asking. And don't forget to ask for help beyond yourself. There's a whole universe of options waiting to bless you in ways you haven't thought about. Remember the second part of this secret is trust.

**After asking, trust the answer to come.
And when it does, repeat the first secret—be grateful!**

CHAPTER 17

THANKSGIVING

O ne morning in November while driving to Mom and Dad's home, I was lost in thought as I reviewed the system of care I had pieced together. I couldn't imagine how my parents could possibly stay in their own home without all the extra help, and I felt sincerely grateful that the new routine seemed to be flowing pretty smoothly with no subsequent crises.

In addition to contemplating the magnitude of supervising a staff of people, I paused to jot a mental note about the importance of saying "thank you" to each person who cared for Mom and Dad that day, and every day, because I knew it was physically impossible for me to care for them alone.

Before leaving the hospital, the care-coordinator had given me a list of additional appointments for my parents. Some of them required trips to doctors' offices and others, including the visiting nurse and occupational therapist, were scheduled in my parents' home. Since my dad voluntarily stopped driving, all transportation was left to me, adding even more hours to an already packed agenda. At least I had people in place to help with most of the day to day in-home responsibilities.

Nearing my parents', a sudden, deep sigh escaped my body. Even before the day began, the stress and fatigue from the preceding weeks threatened to immobilize me like a flat tire. Continuing to breathe or move seemed temporarily optional as I let down in the aftermath of emergencies, the hospital, and all the preparations to care for Mom and Dad. More than once I caught myself saying out loud, "Breathe... just breathe. Just remember to keep breathing..."

Pulling into the driveway I snapped back into the present, remembering that it was a new day with a long list of things to do. I inhaled, anticipating the day's schedule, and opened the door. With as much cheer as I could muster I said, "Well, how are you both doing today? Did you eat breakfast yet?"

Smiling, my mom responded, "Oh yes, we ate some breakfast and took our pills." And as an afterthought she added, "You just missed the nurse."

I quickly pulled out my calendar where I tracked all the to dos for the day and as I was checking the appointment time, Dad said, "Well, she was running early, so she just came on over."

"Dad, did you think about calling me so I could talk to her?"

"No, we handled it just fine."

Trying not to be irritated, I turned toward Mom and said, "I see. What did she say about you?"

Mom looked at me in a rather puzzled way and said, "Well, I couldn't really hear anything she said, but she was really nice and I really liked her a lot."

Glancing Dad's direction, I hoped for a clearer report.

"I couldn't understand her either. She talked pretty fast and not very loud," he said. "We must be doing just fine."

Both of my parents appeared to be completely cognizant and looked considerably younger than their chronological ages of 90. If people spoke to them softly or quickly, their comprehension was nonexistent. Without being present, I had no idea whether I needed to make any adjustments, and trying to get information from the visiting nurse or therapist after an appointment usually proved to be frustrating. Organization was crucial to keep the home-care system functioning, but didn't account for people who arrived early and didn't notify me of a schedule change. Sometimes I simply had to accept the fact that I couldn't read minds or be in multiple places at once!

Managing the staff, grocery shopping, meal preparation, home visits, medications and appointments with multiple doctors filled my every waking moment. Verbally rehashing details after physically coping with everything was impossible, yet SANCTIMONIOUS SHIRLEY, EXHAUSTED TERESA, and WEAK WANDA expected reports from me. Their inability to understand the scope of what was taking place was evident and my silence further angered them.

Thanksgiving arrived, and our son came home for a visit. Seeing him was balm to my weary soul and his presence, medicine to his grandparents' bones. Our celebration was a wonderful day for my family of three. I prepared our meal in my own home, and we enjoyed the day together. EXHAUSTED TERESA and WEAK WANDA came from other towns and spent the day with Mom and Dad. Of course, I was expected by my sisters to attend their meal and spend the day with them. The fact that I chose otherwise added to the widening gap between them and me. They needed to spend time with our parents without me and I certainly needed a break.

Since entering the hospital in October, I had been with our parents multiple times every day for 45 consecutive days. My other three surviving sisters had spent a total of 8 days between them in the presence of our parents while the caregiving staff still remained on duty. EXHAUSTED TERESA, once catching my attention, remarked quite adamantly, "When any of us visit Mom and Dad, we're on 24 hour duty and that, indeed, is much more difficult than anything that you are doing." Regardless of their disappointment in me, I was thankful because we had made it to Thanksgiving. After spending one day with Mom and Dad, the two sisters returned to their lives and my life with our parents resumed.

Three days later, just before our son returned to California, we joined my parents for a traditional Sunday night supper of tomato soup and popcorn. Mom and Dad ate well just as they had been doing since their hospital stay ended. I did not realize, however, until later that our son hardly ate a bite. Instead he had been studying his grandparents' faces and recording their voices in his memory.

When the caregiver arrived for the night shift, Mom and Dad were tired and ready to go to bed. My son gave them each a hug and I noticed his long embraces.

"Bye, Poppie. I love you," he said looking deeply into my dad's eyes.

"Nite, Nonnie. I'll talk to you soon."

In unison, my parents responded, "Nite."

"Always remember how proud we are to be your grandparents and how much we love you!" said my dad.

As we sat in the car after leaving Mom and Dad, my son dissolved in tears.

"Mom, I had no idea how much everything had changed until I saw them," he said.

"I know. It's not easy to see," I said softly.

The truth of what was happening had become a glaring reality my son could not ignore. As hard as it was to watch, I was glad that he did not run away from his feelings.

Haltingly, he continued, "It doesn't feel like much time has gone by since I used to watch cartoons in their bedroom after school. I was just a little kid, but it seems like yesterday. I always felt like they loved me and wanted me to be there."

"Do you remember how they always enjoyed your school activities?" I asked.

"Yeah. And my baseball games. And coming with you and Dad to parents' weekend at camp. Remember how hot it was? They about cooked!"

Nodding with a smile, I said, "It was hot. No doubt about that! But, they wouldn't have missed that opportunity for anything in this world."

My son recounted his memories—past and present. I watched him experience the sadness he felt about not knowing if he would see them again and I listened to the gratitude he felt for his grandparents' valuable contribution to his life. From that moment, Thanksgiving would forever remind us both of the significant events and relationships we shared with people who loved us so deeply.

REFLECTION

TOMATO SOUP, POPCORN & SLIDES

Traditions are as varied as the people who practice them. When I was a child, Sunday night suppers in my family frequently consisted of tomato soup and popcorn, followed by a slide show of my dad's photos projected on a screen. How I loved both of those activities, especially when our extended family spent time with us. Those unique suppers came about because it gave my mom a break from cooking. The after-supper slide show was an alternative to television with its two available stations. I remember the laughter at the slide shows—family adventures recorded by my dad on Ektachrome film—the taste of the hot tomato soup and the wonderful aroma of popcorn.

How grateful I am for tradition and attached memories to something as simple as tomato soup, popcorn and slides.

What is a favorite tradition you recall? Think about the sights, sounds and smells housed in that tradition. Remembering is good. Sharing it is even better. Telling the story reinforces the significance of the tradition.

Try to recall a tradition in your family. If you cannot think of a positive tradition, why not create some for yourself? Go to the movies on New Year's Day. Eat lunch at a nice restaurant every Wednesday. Have a cup of coffee every afternoon with your special someone.

The secret to a tradition? Keep doing it!

What we remember from childhood we
remember forever—permanent ghosts,
stamped, inked, imprinted, eternally seen.

– Cynthia Ozick

CHAPTER 18

A DIFFERENT CHRISTMAS

Early in December my dad's eighty-six year old brother, who lived many states away, sent a letter asking if he might come for a visit. None of us had seen him in more years than I could remember because he had spent a long time taking care of his wife who was slowly stolen away by the thief of dementia. After a painful decision and moving her into a nursing home, my uncle really needed a change of scenery. I immediately phoned to assure him that his visit was just what we all needed. Seeing my uncle after so many years was wonderful. Watching him with my dad was even better as they spent time talking together and sharing brother stuff. We all enjoyed the break in our routine during that week until my uncle returned to his home and our life together continued.

Christmas neared, and I felt paralyzed. Trying to open the boxes of lights and garland to decorate my home as well as my parents' required energy, a commodity I possessed little of. Everyone around me was busy with the hustle and bustle of the season, while I continued to juggle the details of running two households, manage my parents' care and their money issues, while still trying to maintain my lagging design business.

On December 23, I finally dragged myself to the mall. Emotions engulfed me as I made my purchases. Tears welled and retreated. Was this our last Christmas together? I tried to stay in the moment but instead got lost in my thoughts, as they bounced from reliving the events of the past few weeks to foretelling a future that seemed beyond my comprehension, and then back to the overwhelming current situation. Defining my feelings was impossible. I had no clarity, just wandering thoughts and nameless emotion.

Christmas morning my husband and I packed our car with a few presents and food and traveled to my parents' house. Previous holidays were spent at our home, including the year when snowy weather prevented Dad from driving. That year, our son still living with us, drove to Mom and Dad's and brought them back to our house so we could have our celebration together just like all the other years. This Christmas, the first without our son, certainly would be different for all of us. A new type of celebration—a different celebration—was quite a change for everyone.

As we began sharing our gifts I was surprised to learn that a few days before Christmas, Mom and Dad had convinced one of their caregivers to take them to a nearby drugstore where they made some small purchases. The rest of their gifts came from Dad's desk and Mom's cupboards. Dad discovered some peculiar items he had purchased while watching tv infomercials which he gave to my husband. Mom gave me a milk pitcher and a bowl that I remembered from my childhood. It was one of the best times that we celebrated together with the most memorable gifts, indeed.

Our meal, prepared by a local business that specialized in holiday foods, was good, although different than our usual homemade fare. Watching my parents savor every bite, I realized that just being together for one more holiday was all that really mattered. When I allowed myself to notice, the day was simultaneously strange and wonderful.

Mom and Dad, dressed in pajamas and robes, surrounded by oxygen and medical equipment, still found reason to celebrate the season. And so did I.

REFLECTION

HOLIDAYS

While caregiving, the holidays can tip you over the edge! In addition to caregiving responsibilities, the approaching celebration and activities pile on additional pressure as well as self-imposed and family expectations. As the pressure dramatically ramps up during the holidays, you may have to make some choices. Balance is key. Create a list of things that are non-negotiable: maintaining some kind of traditional activities for your kids or mailing gifts to grandchildren. Make another list of all the things you would like to do. Then, begin the task of simplifying. Figure out what can be eliminated or pared down in order to release some of the stress.

Try lowering your expectations. Instead of cooking a big dinner, order one. There are lots of restaurants and grocery stores with staff that happily prepare nice meals for a very reasonable cost. Instead of extensively decorating your home, hang a wreath on your door and place a seasonal plant on your table. Instead of shopping for gifts, purchase or make cards and write a letter to each person of value, telling them what they mean to you. Simplify life as much as you can.

If you can find some balance during the holidays, you may still be able to enjoy the special occasion.

A new way to celebrate might just begin a new tradition.

It is the sweet, simple things of life which are the real ones after all.

– Laura Ingalls Wilder

.

CHAPTER 19

HOSPITAL, AGAIN

One Monday morning after the holidays, I reviewed the day's schedule as I drove to my parents'. I had already fixed dinner for Mom and Dad, so I could check that off my list. I needed to remember to look at the caregivers' notes to see if anything required immediate attention or additional supplies. Making adjustments to my running list of tasks had become second nature in the ten weeks I had been caring for my parents.

Also on the calendar for the day was one of Mom's frequent and usually painful blood tests. Afterward, our reward—a special coffee drink—an "Ooh La La!" Mom called it. When I became Mom and Dad's caregiver, I decided that anytime the day began with a disagreeable activity, we would do something enjoyable before going back home. It only took one time for Mom's "Ooh La La!" to become a greatly anticipated ritual!

With my tentative plan figured out, I opened the door and greeted my parents. "Good morning. Did you sleep well last night?"

As always, Mom's eyes brightened when she saw me. She nodded and glanced at my dad. He was finishing his morning medication, and after swallowing the last of his eight pills, he said, "Like most nights. I don't think I slept much. But, I feel pretty good." He continued, "Oh, while we're out, I need to get my hair cut. The barber can fit me in at 11:00."

The first problem with my dad's plan was his timing. He had scheduled his hair cut at the same time as Mom's blood test. The second problem was the location because the appointments were on opposite sides of town. I had not figured out how to be in two places at the same time although, that seemed to be getting more common as I tried to juggle all of our lives. Fortunately, most doctors run late, enabling us to get Dad's hair cut as well as Mom's blood test and then our treat before returning home.

As Dad grew a bit stronger, with determination he helped my mom by assuming some of the evening kitchen duties. As long as meals were cooked, they could heat and eat. I assumed the responsibility for planning adequate nutrition and cooking their evening meal after I realized my parents had been eating lots of dry cereal for several months prior to entering the hospital. When I discovered their cereal routine, I tried to contain my shock as I asked Dad, "Why are you eating so much cereal these days?"

Rather flatly Dad responded, "Because it's easy and we don't have to figure out what to fix to eat."

No wonder they enjoyed my menu choices and the food my sisters prepared when they came to visit! Lunchtime delivery of meals-on-wheels was not their favorite, but Mom and Dad kept their fussing about the food to a minimum as they always enjoyed visiting with the person who brought their meal.

Late that afternoon, I left Mom and Dad's. My next stop: the grocery store—again. I forgot to take my cell phone into the store and when I returned to my car, calls from my husband were waiting for me. The message; "Your dad called. He's not doing well, and wondered if you could go back to their house." Consumed by growing anxiety, I drove back to my parents' home.

I found Mom and Dad just as I'd left them, in their recliners. I asked what happened and the story unfolded.

"Well, I was helping Mother by heating the food in the microwave. All of a sudden something happened to my legs and they wouldn't hold me up anymore," said my dad.

Mom, still a bit anxious, said, "Yes, but it was amazing! He grabbed the edge of the sink and held on tight and that way he didn't fall to the floor."

Apparently there was no warning before the event and Dad couldn't actually tell at the time whether or not he was hurt. He managed to get himself into the living room to his recliner although his legs "did not feel right" to him.

I asked, "What does **not feel right** mean? Hurting? Are you having difficulty walking?"

"I don't know how to describe it. They just don't feel right," he said.

As we continued our conversation, I noticed how pale Dad appeared to be. Other than the weakness in his legs and a grayish pallor, Dad didn't seem noticeably different from my earlier visit. He walked a bit unsteadily into the bedroom where he changed into his pajamas, ready to retire for the night. After tucking him in, I wrote a note to the night caregiver asking her to call if anything changed. Another sleepless night followed as I wondered what had happened to my dad.

Tuesday morning was ushered in with an early phone call from the morning caregiver.

"Your dad's legs are really bad—barely functioning. You need to get him to his doctor right now!" she said, emphatically.

"Ok, thank you for calling. I'm on my way," I said, trying to avoid sounding annoyed by the tone in her voice.

The frustration of people with good intentions telling me what to do, as though I didn't have a brain, started more than one day on a stressful note and today was no exception. If Dad couldn't walk, how could I manage to help him move around? I had to figure out how I was going to get him from the house into the car and then into the doctor's office. I decided that the time for a wheelchair had arrived. When I stopped by the medical pharmacy, the assessment specialist probed our situation and determined that we needed a transfer chair, something I knew nothing about.

With a quick lesson about the chair and explicit instructions to bring back Medicare and insurance information as soon as possible, I left to collect Dad. Mom and Dad's caregiver had managed to get Dad into his car before I arrived. I moved the wheelchair from one car to the other and my dad and I began our day. The remainder of Tuesday, like so many other days, blurred as time simultaneously sped up and screeched to a halt.

At the doctor's office I found someone to help me transfer Dad from his car to the wheelchair as I was not equipped to handle his 170 pounds alone. As soon as we were escorted into an examination room, Dad announced, "I need to go to the bathroom, *immediately!*" I had absolutely no idea how to handle that situation, a fact that seemed ludicrous in hindsight. Not only was I not prepared, neither was the staff at the doctor's office and that was even more ludicrous! The day that didn't start well, just got worse, but just in the nick of time, one of the nurses came to Dad's rescue.

After waiting for what seemed like an eternity and finally seeing the doctor, there was no diagnosis, and as so often happened with medical appointments, we were sent to another doctor—this time a neurologist.

As we returned to the car, gratefully, I realized that Dad was regaining a bit of control in his legs which helped make the transfer into the car easier. Finding an unfamiliar building and trying to reassure my dad regarding a doctor neither of us knew, occupied my attention and briefly distracted us both from worrying about what had happened to his legs. Again, I had to transfer Dad from his car into the chair. It seemed to be getting a little easier, as I became less afraid of hurting either of us. At the neurologist's office I was given at least a dozen pages to fill out just as Dad whispered, adamantly, that he had to go to the bathroom again. This time, the staff in the doctor's office was busy, leaving me alone to solve the problem. My dad and I reached a whole new level of trust and intimacy that day!

During the interview process, Dad gave the neurologist much inaccurate information—not because he was intending to deceive the doctor, but because he was seemingly unaware of what happened to him during the October hospital stay. Stunned into silence, I didn't know whether to correct him or just hope that the list of medications and the first physician's chart would reveal the truth. The neurologist decided to send Dad to the hospital for additional tests, compounding our growing apprehension by being shuffled around without any answers.

Back we went to the car, transferred from the wheelchair, again, and drove to the hospital for the neurologist-ordered MRI. There, I transferred Dad back to the chair once again and wheeled him inside where I was afraid to leave him alone while parking the car. For some illogical reason, I was afraid that they would not keep him at the hospital but also afraid that they would. My fears weren't always rational when fatigue took over. My anxiety and Dad's uneasiness mounted with each passing hour throughout the day.

As we sat waiting for some kind of decision, I noticed the minister from my parents' congregation had arrived for his usual hospital visitation. It was comforting to see a familiar face as he acknowledged me and my dad. The minister compassionately expressed concern for our uncertain situation, somewhat soothing my mounting fears as I anticipated what caring for Dad might entail if his legs didn't get back to normal. Silently, I repeatedly pleaded with God for the hospital staff to keep him and give me some time to figure things out.

A couple of hours later, Dad was indeed admitted to the hospital. After settling him in a room on the third floor, Dad said, "Thank you for all of your help today. I couldn't have done this without you. I think you'd better get home to your mother and tell her that I'm getting better."

"Okay, I'll get going then. You're in good hands and I'm only a phone call away if you need me," I said. "I'll be back in the morning and if Mom feels up to it, I'll bring her with me. Try to get some rest."

"I will. Give your mother a kiss for me," said my dad as he gave my hand a squeeze.

When I arrived at Mom and Dad's house, I found Mom, nearly frantic with worry. Giving her what little information I knew was all I could do. Calming her fears as best I could, I settled her for the night with the overnight caregiver. After an incredibly long and emotional day, I collapsed into my car and headed back toward my own home. The only noise during my trip across town came from the words tumbling around in my mind.

"Dad... Mom... waiting... more adjustments... home... tired... home..."

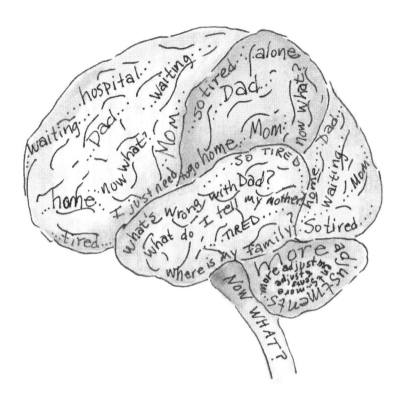

Hard things are put in our way,
not to stop us, but to call out our
courage and strength.

– Author Unknown

REFLECTION

WHEELCHAIRS

I don't know who invented the wheel, but I can tell you that I am certainly thankful for that creative soul. Wheels, attached to anything, make moving less taxing — allowing you to move objects much heavier than would be otherwise possible.

Another person to be thanked is the one who thought of attaching wheels to a chair. Through the years, wheelchairs have developed from most basic to highly sophisticated pieces of machinery, creating independence where none before existed.

There are some pretty fancy walkers with wheels on the market, too. The simplest walker usually sports a pair of tennis balls on its back legs so that the patient can push it without the rubber coated legs stuttering against the floor. More elaborate walkers have wheels, hand brakes, and a seat that covers a carrying basket. Be aware that with more features comes an operational learning curve, so choose carefully.

An array of wheelchairs may be purchased through a medical pharmacy. We used three different types of chairs during my caregiving experience. First came the basic chair that Medicare and insurance supplied. It was a fine chair for use in the house and seemed fairly comfortable. But, boy was it heavy to lift in and out of the car!

Next came the transfer chair that had four small wheels instead of two large rear and two small front wheels like the Medicare chair. A transfer chair is used primarily for transporting a patient to and from the car and is lighter weight than a regular wheelchair because of its smaller wheels. The disadvantage of the transfer chair is lack of comfort as it is not engineered for long term use. And, it is still somewhat awkward to repeatedly lift in and out of the car.

The third chair I discovered was a wonderful lightweight folding transfer chair that fit easily in the car. Even after several stops during a busy day of appointments, I maintained the strength to handle the chair and still had room beside it in the car for groceries. We used the Medicare chair inside the house and the lightweight folding chair for appointments.

Keep your options open and notice anything that makes the job easier and keeps you and your patient or family member safe.

CHAPTER 20

NOW WHAT?

The week drifted into a reminiscent time warp. I lost track of everything again as I stayed with Dad in the hospital. I met a new care-coordinator, more doctors, and finally heard the diagnosis. **A stroke**. The stroke was unlike anything I was familiar with as it affected the lower half of Dad's body rather than his right or left side. Trying to understand what had happened and what we could expect, in addition to Dad's failing heart took the strength from my own legs. The pendulum of emotions swung from confusion and fear to utter sadness and back to fear again.

The days dragged by as, once again, we waited for the unknown. During the hospital ordeal, Dad and I connected in a way that I never expected. As I sat with him, we didn't talk a lot, but holding his hand and just being with him somehow spackled the cracks between us. Those days together allowed me to embrace my dad's unspoken blessing and accept the passing of his mantle to me, uniquely bonding us from that moment.

Once again, my sisters were absent. Mom, Dad and I needed their help and support, but instead each of them remained in their own homes awaiting information from me or my terrified mother.

My resentment for them mounted, augmented by exhaustion. I was left to make all decisions about Dad, care for Mom, as well as the task of communicating with the family to explain and justify my actions.

After another week in the hospital, my dad's legs appeared to be regaining balance and strength, yet his heart was steadily declining and I had to face the fact that the doctors had nothing available to help him. With the care-coordinator's input, I decided that if my dad improved enough to be cared for at home, that is just what would happen. All I had to do was figure out what adjustments had to be made in order to accomplish the goal. As I drove back to my mother that evening, I knew that we had to talk about the impending reality.

I found Mom in her living room, writing desk on her lap, trying to write a letter to someone. Her handwriting, always so strong with the perfectly formed letters of a long-ago school teacher, required effort now. She placed her project to the side and with a somewhat empty look, asked, "What's going on?"

"Mom, I'm planning to do everything I can to bring Dad back home. It's pretty clear that things aren't going to get a lot better for him, but I think I should bring him home to be with you."

Tears began to spill as she quietly said, "He may not be with me much longer. Is that right?"

"Mom, I don't know for sure. I'm not sure of anything right now."

"Ok."

After a long pause, she continued, "I think he may not survive this. I just want you to bring him home to me and I'm going to take care of him."

In that moment a silent strength arose within my mother. She had a new mission—to take care of her beloved as long as possible. My job was to bring him home.

REFLECTION

EXPECTATIONS FROM FAMILY

According to the ***Thorndike-Barnhart Student Dictionary***, **Family** is defined as a group of related people, tribe or clan. Absent from the definition is the concept of perfection or guarantee that related people will support one another.

If you find yourself caring for a parent, brace yourself. Quite possibly, it may be a bumpy ride! I say that not to discourage you but to give you the benefit of experience. My parents always described our family as perfect, a story I believed for many years. The truth is that no family is perfect and should caregiving responsibilities find you, any imperfections are guaranteed to surface.

Tension within the family can come from a variety of sources with communication nearly always being the common denominator. Each person interprets the spoken and written word from her own perspective. Disagreements happen due to the inability to understand the words accurately or because opinions are fiercely protected.

Fear also influences opinions and fuels the embers of disagreement. Don't ignore others' observations, but don't be swayed by them, either. When you have a moment, consider the ideas of the others. There might be relief offered by a thought from someone who is neither physically nor mentally spent. Having said that, I also give you permission to carry on with your own plan or system. After all, *you* are the one in the trenches of caregiving. They are sitting on the sofa doling out opinions and orders. If you can think of it, an appropriate response might be…

"That's an idea worth considering," or "You have a point. Thank you for sharing it with me."

Whatever you do, do not attempt to justify your actions as your words can be your undoing. You think that you are explaining how carefully you've thought through your plan, but the listener may hear with ears that want to turn your words against you. Practice saying the sentences that recognize her words, but never promise to implement their orders.

If you have been a caregiver for any length of time, be confident that you are enough to do this difficult and lonely job. You are enough, regardless of the opinions, however well intentioned, of others.

On the other hand, should you have a supportive family, or even one supportive family member, you are the exception to most families. Be grateful and take any offered support.

Just remember… you are enough!

CHAPTER 21

PROMISE AND PERMISSION

The morning after I brought Dad home from the hospital, Mom called me to say that he was not feeling at all well. My nagging intuition insisted that I visit Dad and spend some time alone with him.

Finding Dad awake and resting in his bed, I struggled to find my voice. Sitting beside him, I asked, "How are you feeling this morning?"

"Oh, I'm so-so," he sighed, as a tear silently rolled from his eye on to the pillow that cradled his head. "Really tired of all of this and worried about your mother. She's having a hard time with everything."

We stayed there in silence—just being together for a few moments.

Holding his hand, the heavy words finally left my mouth. "You know, Dad, you can trust me to be sure that Mom is okay. I will take care of her, no matter what."

He responded quietly, "I know."

Studying and caressing my dad's hand, I knew there was one more important conversation that the still, small voice in my heart insisted upon. "Dad, I know that this is getting to be really tough for you. If staying here becomes too hard, it's okay to let go."

I held my dad as we both allowed our emotions to surface. After what seemed like several hours, he told me that he was not ready to leave just yet. I was comfortable with his response. At least I had said the words aloud to him and hoped they carried calm to his soul.

During the following few weeks I watched Mom experience a renewed sense of purpose and increased strength as she doted on my dad and met his needs, as best she could. Some days were better than others. Most nights were difficult when Dad's heart pain was significantly worse and his level of anxiety escalated. Often my mom would pass the hours by reading to Dad. Although her eyesight was clouding, she still managed to read the newspaper, column by column, or inspirational short stories she found in the stack of magazines beside their bed. Amazingly, dawn nearly always brought ease and comfort for them both.

And so the nights and days continued.

REFLECTION

CONVERSATIONS

Difficult subjects sometimes need to be discussed. You might be asked by others to deliver bad news—news of someone's death, a life-altering diagnosis, or even the necessity for a change in residence. Each uncomfortable conversation carries the potential for unleashed emotions. My advice? No matter how difficult or emotional, **don't leave words left unsaid.** People, if capable of understanding, deserve information. Often, they are much stronger than we realize.

The toughest conversation may be the one in which you give someone permission to let go of life. And, it may be a one-sided conversation if the other person can no longer speak. Say the words anyway. He needs to know **YOU** will be okay or that someone else he is hesitant to leave will be cared for.

Words are powerful. They carry courage, condemnation, reassurance or permission. Just don't leave the words unspoken or expect someone else to do the talking. There is a reason that you feel that tug in your heart or the sense of urgency that won't let you go to sleep. Choose your words wisely as they may be the ones that bring freedom from pain or suffering. It's tough, but I know you can do it and if you listen to that voice inside, you will know exactly the right time and the right words. I didn't say this was an easy thing to do. As is so often the case, the right thing to do is seldom easy. Take a deep breath and do it.

Be Strong!

poWerFul
cOurage
Reassurance
FreeDom
permiSsion

CHAPTER 22

FEELING LIKE AN ONLY CHILD
WITH SIBLINGS

After my dad's hospitalization, granddaughter *MANIPULATED MICHELE* as well as *SANCTIMONIOUS SHIRLEY*, and *WEAK WANDA* arrived for short visits. Each one uniquely expressed her observation about how my parents were progressing, leaving me speechless most of the time.

MANIPULATED MICHELE rarely said anything of substance, but always agreed with whomever else offered an assessment of any situation. I had never before realized how easily influenced she was by those around her. Much to my shock, *MANIPULATED MICHELE*'s lack of self confidence and the close proximity of her home played a key role in our family in years that followed.

SANCTIMONIOUS SHIRLEY suggested that I needed to pray more, so Dad might be healed. Her explanation for any illness or difficulty in life amounted to a lack of doing two things — sufficiently praying and reading the Bible.

WEAK WANDA just wanted to go back home. Her visits with our parents were obligatory, at best. From the moment she arrived, she smiled, held Dad's hand, tried to ignore his condition and rattled on about her need to return home.

The family visits annoyed me as I observed their involvement with Mom and Dad. Each one performed a few tasks to quell her conscience, and delivered additional opinions before leaving. Within me, the pendulum of emotion continued swinging wildly from fear and irritation with them to my gut-wrenching need for my life to return to **normal**.

Each family member enjoyed a life of her own, including jobs and families, augmented by social lives and activities. Mom and Dad were my life, along with my husband and a formerly thriving business. At least a ton of paperwork waited on my desk and just walking past the piles stoked a fire of mounting frustration. In spite of the actions and attitudes of my family members, I still found it difficult to accept that I, alone, was taking care of all things concerning my parents with nothing but judgment from the others.

Following their brief visits, even conversations that involved the names of my sisters caused the hair to stand up on the back of my neck. In time, I learned to acknowledge my feelings and accept that although I had siblings, in many ways I was an only child.

REFLECTION

NORMAL - A DRYER SETTING

If your life suddenly shifts, I can guarantee that the desperation to get back to normal will consume your thoughts. You long for your routine… your stake in the ground… your anchor that promises a wildly rocking boat will not capsize. You just want to get back to **normal!**

Brace yourself. **NORMAL** is nothing more than a setting on your clothes dryer.

We all exist in an illusion we label as **normal**.

As a caregiver, you may have a system in place that has been working for you and your family member. If it's working smoothly enough, you might resume some of your former activities. You are almost lulled into thinking that **"things are finally getting back to normal."** And that's usually when something falls apart right in front of your eyes and the life you knew as **normal** evaporates.

When you can take a breath, picture a clothes dryer set on **normal**. Remind yourself over and over that **normal** only lives in the dryer. You are living this life, however unfamiliar it may feel.

Know that you are not alone in feeling desperate to return to normal. Anyone who has become an unexpected caregiver has felt this way. Take a breath. Relax and remember...

Stay anchored in the present, not lured by an illusion of the past, or fear of the future. This is where you live.

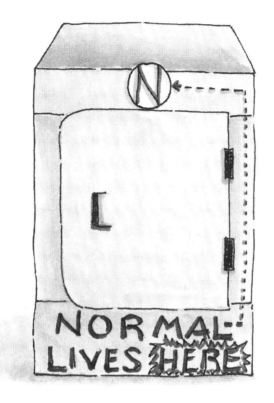

As we struggle to make sense of things,

life looks on in repose.

– Author Unknown

CHAPTER 23

PIANO

Just as I thought I was surely losing my mind, a new piano partner entered my life. She and I were asked to perform at a banquet to provide dinner music as people milled in, locating their seats. It certainly wasn't performing on stage for an audience, but at least it was something. I had not played the piano nor performed for anyone in several years, so I welcomed the opportunity with more than a little trepidation. Practicing the piano provided a distracting and comfortable place away from endless schedules and blindsiding events. Stealing an occasional hour for myself, I connected with the music. Learning was not as easy as it used to be, but my necessary concentration brought a wonderful reward—escape!

My brain vacillated between complete absorption in the music and micro managing details that were waiting somewhere. In spite of my lack of concentration at times, I felt my powerful emotions diffuse for a while. Rejuvenated by playing the music, sitting on the bench, stretching out my fingers and allowing the simple joy of the notes to penetrate my soul, I received a gift of remembering who I really was. In those moments, my role of caregiver dissolved, problems evaporated and I felt years drop away as I embraced that gift with abandon!

The day of the banquet arrived and I surprised my parents by making arrangements with the caregivers on duty to take them to the location where my partner and I were performing. Not only did Mom and Dad get to hear our music, they were greeted by many people whom they had not seen for months. Watching them smile as they enjoyed the moment propped me up with new determination to continue our journey with as much grace as possible.

When the day came to a close, I realized how stimulated and tired we all were. Once again, I was reminded by the world around me to stay connected to each moment. Emergencies might happen again. Routines might have to be repeatedly adjusted. My family members were going to behave exactly as they chose and no amount of fretting would change anything other than depleting my own valuable resources.

My piano partner, who grew to love my parents almost as much as I did, proved to be one of my most cherished sources of inspiration. One day when I felt tethered to life by a mere thread, she said, "Hey, I found this for you! I don't know who wrote it first, but I keep seeing it. Maybe it will help." The piece of paper she handed me contained the following words: **Time is a gift. That's why it's called the present.** Exactly when I needed it, I found my new motto.

The past is behind, learn from it.

The future is ahead, prepare for it.

The present is here, live it.

– Thomas S. Monson

REFLECTION

DISTRACTIONS

Do you have a distraction from your caregiving responsibilities? You need something to give your thoughts and physical body a break from the enormity of caring for someone. Although you never completely get away from the situation, distracting yourself—however fleeting—may help you survive.

Just a word of warning...

Consciously choose your distraction or something may choose you. Be aware that some distractions pose danger. Abuse of alcohol fits this category. It begins innocently as a way to relax. In time the body requires more alcohol to achieve the same state of relaxation. If left unchecked, a dependence on the distraction may well occur. Stay conscious. Keep your head in the game and know that all along the path you are walking, you choose to be present or distracted. If you have any tendency toward addiction, caregiving may reveal or magnify your vulnerability.

Suggestions for constructively dealing with distractions:

- Set time limits. "I'll spend one hour on the computer." Or, "I'll watch TV until _____."
- Create simple yet achievable goals. Example: exercise at least 2 days each week (a great distraction with positive side effects.)
- Play a musical instrument at least once a week.
- Write in a journal every day — even if all you can manage to write is, "Thank you for getting through another day."
- Try visual journaling. Get a sketch book or just some blank paper and some kind of drawing tools like oil pastels, crayons, a child's watercolor set, colored pencils, etc. Quiet your mind, as best you can, and ask yourself how you feel. Then, pick up your chosen drawing tool and begin doodling. Don't feel any pressure to draw something or to create some sort of illustration. Just doodle. Just putting color or shapes on paper can help release emotions. Give it a try!

Distractions can be very positive unless they overwhelm your life. Use a distraction for its intended purpose — to give you a break. Don't forget to come back!

Stay connected to yourself. Be present.

CHAPTER 24

SAYING GOOD-BYE

My dad's younger brother arranged another visit with us in March— this time to celebrate his eighty-seventh birthday. Our time together in December was so good for all of us that I indeed looked forward to his return. He understood the process of caregiving, as he had been the sole caregiver for his wife for more than four years, and his approval regarding the care of my parents meant a lot to me.

Our visit began wonderfully, followed by uncomfortable tension as my uncle expressed his observation of my stress level. With the best of intentions, he advised and then pressured me to make changes.

"You just can't keep doing things this way. I know that you're trying to do everything possible to provide the best care for your parents and I know how much you love them, but I can see what it's doing to you," he said to me with a soft, yet firm tone.

My uncle overheard my conversations as I answered early phone calls from my mother each morning. As reality scared them, Mom and Dad wanted me to be present even more. When they called, I went to them, calming them as best I could.

Later, when I returned home, my uncle scolded me by saying, "I'm telling you, you have to make changes, now! You don't even see what is happening to you."

I adored him, but his words made the situation even more difficult for me to handle.

Dad was spiraling downward, and I had no idea what to change to make anything better for him or for me. I did my best to rationally solve each problem as it arose. Neither Dad nor I hid our fear very well. Mom's feelings were less obvious as she was completely focused on her mission of trying to take care of my dad. Each of us attempted, futilely, to cling to the moment.

The third morning of my uncle's visit, my dad awoke, fearful and in pain. Realizing that the machinery of Dad's body was grinding to a halt, the nurse on duty did everything in her power to soothe his immediate discomfort. In a moment that morning, Dad decided that he was no longer taking his medication— a decision that we all agreed belonged to him. As he further declined throughout the day, Mom became frightened and called me to come to their house. There was nothing I could do but be with them. Somehow, that was enough.

Early the next morning, I took my uncle to stay with my parents while my husband and I attended a day long business meeting for his company. Knowing that my uncle was with my parents, I felt confident about being away for a few hours. I just wanted to escape reality for a little while and retreated behind my wall of stoicism. I planned to resume dealing with my parents' lives when I returned from the brief respite-meeting. The morning caregiver assured me that she would call if the situation with Dad changed, and we went on with our plans.

At the exact moment our meeting concluded, my cell phone rang. It was my uncle calling. "I'm afraid that your father is no longer with us," he said. I don't remember how I responded. I only remember being frozen by his words and clutching my cell phone. The seconds of silence before I told my husband were void of time and space.

I finally managed to whisper, "That was my uncle. My dad just died."

My husband's eyes told me everything I needed to know. I saw and absorbed his unspoken message. "Don't worry. We'll take one step and then another and we'll get through this together."

Propelled into an unfamiliar place, I couldn't think rationally. I didn't know what to do. My mind careened out of control. "I was coming back... I didn't mean to sound like I didn't care... I was going to make him feel better... I just needed a break for a day... I'm so sorry... I'm so sorry..."

I dreaded every minute as my husband and I drove to my parents' home. I couldn't remember if I talked to my dad that morning. I couldn't remember if I told him that I loved him. I just couldn't remember. I felt so sad and guilty and raw. Somewhere in the shock and sadness I vowed never to miss another chance to say, "I love you" or "Thank you" or "You are important to me." I could not relive that day with my dad but I never had to be *too busy* to let another opportunity escape.

We pulled into the driveway and my uncle, tears spilling from his eyes, greeted us. After a long embrace, it was time to enter the house. I found Mom sitting beside my dad. He was lying on his bed where he had gone to rest because he didn't feel like eating lunch. Mom was sobbing, holding my dad's hand. She looked up at me, her eyes pleading for me to do something. Nearly immobilized by the scene, I had to force myself to walk toward the bed. I really didn't want to look at him. I had only seen someone in a casket after the funeral people had prepared them for viewing. This was my daddy and I wanted him to wake up and say, "Hello," just the way he had said that word to me during the past several months.

He was so still. For a moment I really believed that he was going to open his eyes. Instead, he just laid there — still and silent.

We all stayed in the bedroom, together — Mom, Dad, my uncle, my husband and me. Those moments were awful and yet strangely comforting. My father looked peaceful as if there had been no struggle. I believe his struggle happened all the weeks before he left us. Finally, he was free from fear and pain.

When I managed to flip my internal switch back to the place where I could deal with the issues in front of me, new lists poured from my pen. I was afraid that I would forget something important if I didn't write everything on paper. I wasn't quite sure where to begin until logic took control. The first item on my list was deciding whom I had to notify. I picked up the phone, cleared my throat and began the process of calling people.

Somehow my fingers found the correct number for the funeral home and after a short conversation, I was told that everything would be taken care of and someone would be sent to my parents' within the hour. When the men in black suits arrived, once again the couch and chairs were pushed aside to make room for a gurney. My husband took my mother into another room while I answered the suited men's questions and then, they took my daddy away. As I watched him leave, I was overcome by silent screams. "Now what? Now what? Now what?" I had no concept of what would happen next, only that there was no chance of my dad returning home this time. Standing in the kitchen, watching the hearse pull out of the driveway it seemed like an eternity since my parents spent those ten days together in the hospital in October. With a sudden gasp, I realized it had only been five months.

That day in March was my uncle's eighty-seventh birthday and my dad died. In my worst nightmare, I never thought that day could unfold as it did.

I just wanted to crawl out of my skin and into a hole where no one could find me ever again.

I phoned our son, the hardest call I have made to anyone in my life. He is *my heart*, and he was so very far away. I needed him as much as he needed me, and we were so far apart. After telling him about his Poppie, he asked to speak to his grandmother.

"Hi Nonnie... I love you..."

I don't know how he talked to her or what he said, but his voice was exactly what she needed in that moment. After hanging up the phone Mom's voice trailed off as she said, "That sweet boy. I wish I could hug him…"

The phone calls continued and time stopped. People called me about details. People called Mom to express their condolences. The phone rang continuously, no matter where I was.

That night, sleep escaped me entirely. I couldn't swallow anything. Trying to care for myself was impossible. Caring for my mother was my sole focus.

The morning after my father died, Mom and I finalized his funeral arrangements. First, we drove to the funeral home where we confirmed the decisions Dad made years earlier. Next, I drove us to the church where the funeral was to take place. With my mother holding my arm as well as her cane for support, we entered the minister's office. My mother and I wanted my dad's life to be honored, not mourned. We wanted his humanity to be revealed. Most people knew him as professor or elder or teacher, but few people knew him as the dad, husband and grandfather that we knew. Mom and I shared lots of stories with the minister so that he could weave the life of my dad into the tribute of honor we wanted.

Ordering flowers was our last task. When someone passed, ordering funeral flowers was always my dad's first thought. This time, however, they were for him. A man who taught people about the beauty of flowers deserved to have the most beautiful bouquets. For Mom and me, that proved to be the most difficult part of the funeral preparation. Selecting flowers was something we needed to do, and yet it illuminated the glaring realization that this event had really happened.

Just after the arrangements were completed, my family began arriving. Each of them wanted to know what to do. Each of them wanted to help and looked to me for direction. Each of them wrestled with the finality of what had occurred in our family. I had few words for them because I was afraid to begin speaking. I was fearful that I couldn't control my feelings and if I allowed them to vocalize, I would add to the shock my mother was already experiencing.

Dad's funeral was exactly what Mom and I hoped it would be. As we listened and wept, hymns filled the sanctuary, flowers overflowed, the minister beautifully honored my dad and a single handbell tolled.

After the ceremony, my family ate the dinner provided and served by my dear friends. We reminisced about Dad, surrounded Mom with our presence and love, and one day later, everyone — including each of my sisters — went home. In less than 24 hours, it was over and no one even questioned what would happen next in my mother's life. Since the moment of my uncle's phone call telling me of my Dad's passing, I had not stopped thinking about what would happen. Neither had my mother. I can still hear her soft, frightened voice when she asked me,

"What is going to happen to me?"

After a moment I responded, "Mom, I don't know yet, but together, we will figure it out."

REFLECTION

LIFE CELEBRATIONS AND FUNERALS

It's inevitable. Death happens. Funerals are as varied as the people involved. Some need a traditional funeral; complete with hymns, prayers and lots of emotion. Others need a celebration of life service. Some people even opt for no service at all. No choice is right or wrong.

You need to do what feels right in your individual situation. It doesn't matter what anyone thinks you **should** do. If possible, try to consider a plan before the event. Although the service centers around the person who has passed, its purpose is for the benefit of the survivors, allowing some closure and hopefully some peace.

Take some time to think about how you might fulfill your objectives. What do you want to say about your loved one? Are there aspects of the personality that you want to highlight? Are there experiences that you want to share with others? Do you enjoy music and the mood it suggests? Is the beauty and fragrance of flowers important? What about photographs or a powerpoint presentation? Do whatever you need to do for your loved one AND for yourself. If you have been the primary caregiver, the service can be a first step toward your healing.

My choice? I like the idea of celebrating life. I find comfort in uplifting music, beautiful flowers and people who share love and respect for my loved one. You may make a different choice and whatever you decide is perfectly valid.

Now, for the uncomfortable subject of finances. Funerals can be very expensive. I would suggest that you pre-plan and pre-pay as much as possible. If you wait until after the passing to begin making decisions, choices may be overly emotional and even illogical.

No matter how much you try to ignore an approaching passing, you can't stop it. Open your heart as best you can. Stay in the moment. Give recognition and honor to your loved one, while being kind to yourself.

Listen to your heart. You will know what to do.

PART II

REGROUP

RECOGNIZE

REBIRTH

CHAPTER 25

DEATH AND DEALING

I needed time to grasp what had happened in my family, but the world didn't stop to let me regroup, even for a moment. The day that impacted my life in such a powerful way was just another day for each person with whom I interacted. Somehow, I needed to absorb the blow of my father's death, but there was no chance, as caring for Mom continued without interruption. She was now completely dependent on me for everything—her safety, conversation, peace of mind and the never-ending schedule of appointments.

In the aftermath of my dad's death, I lost count of the times I had to say, "My father just died." I found a place within that allowed me to speak without feeling, because my tears had to wait.

The distance between my sisters and me was growing, causing our communication to disintegrate even further. Every time I had to say something about my father's passing, the person on the other end of the phone always said **something**. Sometimes she said, "I'm sorry for your loss," or "I understand." My sisters said **nothing**. I couldn't understand how strangers were more compassionate than my own family. I stuffed my angry feelings, hoping for some kind of miraculous relief from the tension inside me. From some strange, far away place. I lost touch with myself and everything I'd ever known about **family**.

REFLECTION

THE WORLD NEEDS TO STOP!

Any time you experience a shocking event, your world is shaken. Your routine hesitates and then halts as your thoughts tangle into a jumble.

What should you do first? How will you survive an event of such magnitude?

Autopilot can engage, letting you simply go through the motions of living for a while. As luck or fate would have it, this is often a time when decisions have to be made and pressing problems require solutions.

You find yourself in strangely unfamiliar territory, and yet everyone around you is carrying on normal routines. Schools are in session. Bills arrive in the mail with creditors expecting payment while you struggle to hold a pen. Your body needs nourishment in spite of the lack of appetite or awareness of hunger. And then there are the people who don't know what has happened. Innocently, someone asks, "So how are you today?"

— How can the world continue when yours has collapsed?

— I have to tell you, it just does.

— No matter how much you want the world to acknowledge what has happened to immobilize you, it will not.

Keep breathing and putting one foot in front of the other. Ever so slowly, balance will begin to resurface. It takes as long as it takes. One day, you realize that you are becoming a part of the world again—going to work, paying bills, eating a nice meal, enjoying a movie.

The world didn't stop, after all, and that is a very good thing.

You may delay, but time will not.

– Benjamin Franklin

CHAPTER 26

THE IDEA

My mother was overwhelmed by thoughts of her future. She realized that with my father's death, the house was too much for her to think about trying to maintain. She also understood that living alone was not an option as she was completely dependent on other people to help her with even the most basic activities.

I promised my dad in one of our last conversations that I would always care for my mom. I had no concept of how I could honor my promise. If I hired round the clock care for Mom, money would evaporate at an alarming rate. Another option was a nursing home and I just couldn't stand the thought of her being there. No one in my family offered any solution or physical help. Engulfed by thoughts of what would become of my mother, I had to let go of the worry and hope some acceptable solution would show up.

A few days later, it arrived out of the blue, courtesy of my husband. By selling my parents' house and using a portion of the proceeds, we could build a private apartment for Mom on to our home and move her to live with us. The cost of the addition was a consideration, but Mom's resources would be exhausted quickly with any other option. I had to spend money to care for Mom, no matter what, so my decision was based on two things: my mother's safety and my mental health. It seemed that if she were only a few steps away from me, the choice was obvious for both of us.

Indeed we had an idea, but my mother held the final vote. We chose lunchtime and Mom's favorite restaurant to present the building option to her. Her face began to light up with the realization that we wanted her with us, and were willing to create a place just for her. She savored every word, repeating over and over, "Yes, yes I want to live with you! You really want me? Oh, yes, yes! When can we start?" A dream that she had not dared dream allayed her worst fears — living in a nursing home or living with someone other than me.

Finances continued to be a puzzle. Slowly the way became clear as I sorted through papers and gathered information, paving the way for us to begin the project in late April. With a plan in place, I finally felt my breathing ease and deepen a bit as my fear of the future dimmed.

It takes a lot of courage to release the

familiar and seemingly secure,

to embrace the new.

– Alan Cohen

REFLECTION

IT WILL APPEAR

I f you are stumped by not knowing what to do — a position in which most caregivers repeatedly find themselves — just stop for a moment. Stop fretting and worrying, just for now.

Get a piece of paper and make a list of advantages and disadvantages concerning your current quandary. Contemplate each advantage and disadvantage. Write down everything you can think of associated with each advantage and disadvantage. Keep writing until your words are exhausted. Next, look at each thing on your list and feel any emotion that comes up. In your imagination write your feeling on a kite. Set it free and let the wind carry the kite away. Just let the emotion float away with the kite. Repeat the steps for each advantage and disadvantage as long as it takes for the emotions to lessen. The goal is for the feelings to go away for now.

It may seem ridiculous to take your valuable time to do this. This is where I tell you to trust me! **Just do it!**

Next, go do something unrelated to your situation. Take a walk or a nap. Go to the library or have a cup of tea with a friend. An answer will appear. It may suddenly pop in to your thoughts or present itself in a conversation with someone. The ideas and answers are like fish leaping out of the ocean waiting for us to catch them before they disappear beneath the surface again. When something shows up, grab it!

**I can't explain how it works, but it does.
Stay open and watch for the fish.**

CHAPTER 27

THE BUILDING PRESSURE

ascinated, I watched my mother cope with the loss of my dad and embrace her newly discovered independence. She actually seemed to be coming into her own, something I never could have predicted! Mom's decision to move forward as she anticipated a new adventure provided a purpose for her life, and her attitude toward the future inspired everyone around; everyone except her other daughters. Mom had a good appetite, and fresh food seemed to clear her thinking and somewhat increase her physical strength. She was enjoying her life!

Even though Mom was sad to think of leaving the home she shared with my dad, she was thrilled at the prospect of a place being built just for her. Since familiarity is comforting for elderly people, we configured 800 square feet of space to be as much like her current house as possible. We replicated the bay window from her living room, the skylight from her bathroom along with as many other details as we could. My husband was able to plan the bedroom space so that we could place her furniture exactly as it had been in the room Mom shared with my dad, hoping to prevent nighttime disorientation. My mother loved watching each step of the plan evolve.

Decisions had to be made about what to move into Mom's new space and what to do with everything else. The task of sorting and emptying the contents of every room, cabinet, closet and the garage demanded any spare time. My husband, realizing that the garage was my idea of a nightmare, took that project upon himself. Everything was exactly as my dad had left it, including his tools, empty cardboard boxes, and dozens of flower containers. Although he had not been able to work in the garage for months, Dad still somehow managed to collect things and add to his stuff. The endless choices of what to save, what to dispose of and what to give family members were enough to drive us crazy.

Pressure increased dramatically during the weeks following my dad's funeral. My husband arose early every day and before going to work, continued preparing the area for the addition to our home. I was swamped by the paperwork details after my father's death and managing my mother's care, in addition to dealing with their physical possessions. Staying organized was essential, yet very challenging. My aqua plastic folder, always in my arms, was bulging and heavy from the accumulation of papers, notes, and appointments.

The daily routine never slowed and at times I didn't know where I was. Even though I had only my mother to care for, there were regular trips to multiple doctors and pharmacies and grocery stores. Sometimes I forgot what I was shopping for in the grocery store and for whom. Sleep became more elusive than ever and I teetered on the edge of exhaustion, as did my husband.

The distance from sanity to insanity seemed shorter with each passing day. I endeavored to hang on, saved only by the hope that the pressure would end. Soon enough, I believed with all of my being, there would be no more trips across town to collect Mom in order to travel back across town for appointments… no more running, cleaning, and keeping up two separate households… no more worrying about whether my mother would open her door to a stranger or whether she would fall during the few hours she was alone during the day.

I trusted that I could survive, until things changed.

I had to hang on.

REFLECTION

THE WILL TO SURVIVE

I wondered why the toll taken on a family caregiver was so great until a fellow caregiver shared some statistics. Before becoming her husband's caregiver, she worked for an assisted living facility and had the opportunity to observe and count the number of people who interacted with a resident on a regular basis.

A normal day is divided into 3 shifts. Each shift has at least 2 aides to assist the nursing staff for a minimum of 6, plus the nurses. There are at least 2 cooks, 2 dishwashers, 2 servers, people who are in charge of laundry and housekeeping, others in charge of maintenance, at least 1 driver to transport residents to and from appointments, the activities director and the overseers; the administration and finance departments.

If you are the sole caregiver, you fill each of these positions. Do you feel exhausted? If not, at some point you will! I give you these statistics not to discourage you but to applaud you. This is a very demanding time in your life and not to be diminished by others. Your motivation to continue caring for your family member is fueled by love, compassion or a sense of duty. Regardless, it's possible to find the will to survive and complete the caregiving journey. Don't be surprised if your own survival becomes the goal, second only to providing care for your loved one.

And, if you cannot personally carry on with all caregiving responsibilities, there are other options available. **You will always be a caregiver, even if a staff of people replaces you.** Just remember that if you crash and burn, the person you care for may be at the mercy of someone else.

Your survival really is in the best interest of your loved one.

CHAPTER 28

BEGINNING

Finally, a break in the spring rains! We sneaked in the foundation for Mom's apartment by unabashedly begging the concrete contractor for help. Once the footing and slab were poured, the addition grew remarkably quickly. My husband worked tirelessly with subcontractors doing anything possible to hasten the project to completion. He remained steadfastly focused on expediting the building so that I could be in one place, instead of living in my car, traveling to and from my mother's house multiple times each day.

Several times a week, I brought Mom to her new home to see the progress. As she watched the development, her emotions intensified. Never in her life had a space been planned and decorated just for her. From foundation to wallpaper and paint, Mom enjoyed every step of the construction process. She really loved watching her new place become reality and told us so, repeatedly, with the anticipation and excitement of a child.

As the construction was progressing, with Mom's blessing, I continued dismantling her house. We contacted each of my sisters and all of the grandchildren about Mom's desire to share her possessions. Some of them responded positively and some did not.

During those weeks Mom occasionally felt energetic enough to sort things with me, deciding what she wanted to save for herself or give away. The kitchen was the most difficult room for us. She loved her kitchen, and to imagine moving from a wonderful, spacious, country-style kitchen to a tiny kitchenette was beyond her comprehension. I packed everything that she wanted to keep, even though I knew she would not be using most of it. When neither of us could stand the sorting and decision-making any longer, we abandoned the project for a while and traveled across town to her emerging apartment where we sat on her new deck and imagined what living life together would be like.

It always seems impossible until it's done.

– Nelson Mandala

REFLECTION

ANTICIPATION

Do you remember how much fun it is to look forward to something? Anticipating an event or change of some kind can be energizing. It's sometimes even a bit scary.

As long as a person lives, she needs something to anticipate. It might be as simple as the next meal or as complex as waiting for a new place to live. Anticipation may bring out the best in one person and unusual anxiety in another. A spiral into self-absorption is a frequent expression in the elderly and having something to anticipate just might help curb that.

As a caregiver, along with routine duties, you might be well advised to spend some time creating something for your patient to anticipate. It may require energy you think you do not have, but might serve to occupy the thoughts of the person you care for, which could give **you** a little unexpected respite. Talk about an upcoming holiday—or make one up! If your patient is mobile, plan a special trip for a meal or coffee. When someone is housebound, most any excursion is met with joy. If you cannot go places together, think about having someone come to visit. Having someone read to your patient can transport her to far away places, allowing her to forget the aches and pains for a bit. Sometimes children relate to the elderly in a wondrous way. Why not let a child read the story?

Think about building the anticipation for the person you care for at the right time. Only you know when that is. There may be a fine line between creating excitement or anxiety, so use your own judgment.

I know this requires you to balance one more thing, but I think you may find the reward for you and your patient worth the time spent.

CHAPTER 29

THE LETTERS

The first letter arrived just a few weeks after my father's death. Too many of them followed. The letters were authored by *Exhausted Teresa*, whose fingers were never too tired to type. Her letters were supposed to point out "the errors in our thinking" as she questioned the speed with which we were moving.

This was the same woman who, knowing her father's tenuous physical condition, chose to leave the country two weeks before his death, causing her to be absent from his funeral and her family during such a pivotal time. With self-aggrandizing authority she wrote, "According to **all** the books I've read about death and dying, making such momentous decisions regarding one's future after losing a spouse is a grievous error."

My sister wanted our very needy 90-year-old mother "to remain right where she was for a period of at least 6 months, or better yet, one year." *Exhausted Teresa* offered no practical help or acknowledgement of the cost that such a waiting period was bound to have on me and my husband, but rather insinuated that I was only taking advantage of our "helpless" mother.

"Obviously, since you didn't bring this idea up before our father died, your plan is little more than a hidden agenda with secret motives and a way of making sure that you get all their money for yourself," she accused.

The biting words in each letter were leveled at two women: my mother who buried her companion of more than 65 years only weeks before, and me, stressed and stretched nearly to the breaking point.

EXHAUSTED TERESA used distance as her shield from which to shoot the arrows of her venomous accusations. She could no longer be bothered to participate in person and rarely phoned Mom, but didn't pause her destructive epistles for several months. When I ignored her missives, my sister bypassed me and sent them directly to our mother. I encouraged Mom to vent her obvious pain, as best she could, to her journal rather than to my sister. Mom, with arthritic but determined fingers, faithfully recorded her thoughts and feelings about everything EXHAUSTED TERESA wrote, until one letter proved to be too much for her. That one deserved a phone call from Mom.

Her normally calm, soft voice boomed out, leaving a memorable sting behind, "I have kept silent until now, but no longer. I love you, but your words are ridiculous! You obviously think I'm incapable, but I know exactly what I want to do and where I want to live. I cannot stay in this house by myself. It's too much for me and it's too much for your sister to continue handling. You may not approve of my choices, but they are just that... mine! You will do well to thank your sister for taking such good care of your father and me. She has given up her life to make this happen. Perhaps you should deal with your own business and stay out of ours!"

Without entertaining her daughter's response, Mom hung up. I could barely believe my ears! I had no recollection of my mother ever standing up to anyone and I couldn't help but swell with a bit of pride as I observed her newly expressed self-confidence.

As we neared completion of the construction, one extraordinarily ludicrous letter from EXHAUSTED TERESA arrived in my mailbox. My sister had finally pushed me too far and I decided the time had come for her to hear my voice.

"Hello," I said.

I was greeted with momentary silence as EXHAUSTED TERESA determined to whom she was speaking.

"Oh, hello!" my sister said, with enthusiasm that surprised me. "How are you?"

Flatly, I responded, "How I am is irrelevant. Your letters are hurting Mom and they need to stop, now."

EXHAUSTED TERESA'S tone suddenly shifted from one of victory by goading me into a response, to instant spite.

She spewed, "Well, how do you think you're going to make me do that? You're not in charge of me! I can write anything I choose. **You** can't stop me from doing anything."

Calmly I replied, "I don't have to **do** anything. You are the one who needs to do something. And that would be stop sending your typewritten crap."

EXHAUSTED TERESA continued sputtering her loathing and suspicion of me for a few more sentences. My sister repeatedly questioned our mother's ability to think for herself and spit out every vile word she could conjure up about Mom and me. No longer able to contain myself or reason with her, I ended the conversation.

I grew up hearing my family members excuse EXHAUSTED TERESA'S temper tantrums and demands on them by saying, "Well, you know how she is. You just have to ignore her." This time was different. No longer would I make excuses for her behavior or her words. Dad had bequeathed Mom's welfare to me and in spite of my seething overload of emotion, I fully intended to honor his trust, no matter what my sister had decided about me.

ᴀᴀ ᴀᴀ 🍃 ᴀᴀ ᴀᴀ

REFLECTION

OPINIONS

Have you discovered that there is no shortage of opinions in this world? Everyone has one regarding most any subject, just like everyone has a mouth. You can learn a lot about someone by listening to their opinions.

According to the dictionary in my computer, **"an opinion is a view or judgment about something, not necessarily based on fact or knowledge."** Read that again and take it to heart. You might even consider writing the definition on a sticky note and placing it where you often see it.

If you are an active caregiver, opinions will be lobbed your direction by almost anyone, whether they have the best interest of your patient in mind or not. Opinions are personal and usually meant to alter your thinking or behavior in some way. If you have time, consider the opinions of others. If not, file them in the recesses of your mind or zap them with your imaginary delete key!

You are the person on the caregiving front line. Stay in the moment. You cannot afford the luxury of second-guessing every choice you make. Remember that acknowledging the opinionated person is a good idea, as it gives him validation, but you are under no obligation to act upon the opinion.

Continuing the journey with your patient is the goal. Only you know what is best for both of you.

CHAPTER 30

THE BLUR

My life felt like the spin cycle of a washing machine. When I thought that I could not go faster, everything around me sped up. All tasks and responsibilities fell in my lap and everyone looked to me for everything concerning my mother. Care had to be managed for her, translating into ongoing schedule challenges. Money had to come from somewhere for Mom's personal expenses as well as maintaining her household. I was still trying to figure out how much money was available and where my father had put it.

I continued sorting and packing as well as occasionally contacting family members, cajoling them to visit my mother. Mom sensed the mounting pressure but had no capacity to really help. She worried about me and steadily grew more frustrated by the absence of her other daughters. My feeble attempts to hide the stress did not fool her one bit. Neither of us knew what to do to lessen the load.

There was no language to quantify what was happening in my heart nor how fast it was beating. I lost track of the times my pounding heart or a sudden gasp for air jarred me from my tenuous sleep in the night. As I listened, my intuition assured me there would be an end, or at least a change, even though I could not feel or see it.

Life spun faster and faster as one day blurred into the next.

REFLECTION

STOP!

Have you been in a spin cycle? Are you in a spin cycle now? Are you desperate for that cycle to stop? If you are actively caregiving, I bet your answer to at least two of those questions is, "Yes!" Accumulating activities and accelerated thoughts fuel your high-speed spin cycle.

Ready for some good news?

"This too, shall end. It didn't come to stay, it came to pass!"

I do not remember who shared that insight with me or when. I thought it was a crazy statement. As one day became the next, I eventually realized that the essence of that statement was correct. Routines ceased as new ones began. Things changed. Just when I thought I could not stand one more minute of life as it was, something shifted.

While you wait for things to change, try one of the following techniques and see what happens:

Picture an imaginary pressure cooker and put **the cause** of your spin cycle inside. Your pressure cooker might be inside your head or on an imaginary stove. The location isn't important, but the picture is. See it with as much realism as you can. When you feel the pressure accumulating as the stress from too much responsibility builds up, open the valve and let the steam and stress escape. Let the steam carry everything away. Watch it all disappear. Feel the relief. Take a deep breath. Take another one.

What about your hyper-drive head? Do you chase circular thoughts or one annoying mantra that refuses to leave? Try the imaginary pressure cooker again. When the valve opens, let your circular thoughts escape and dissolve.

If the pressure cooker valve refuses to open, try this. Think the word, **"Stop!"** Think it or say it with emphasis. Picture a big red stop sign as you hear the word, **"Stop!"** Repeat if needed to interrupt the thought flow. It's simple, but can be very effective.

Use whatever works. Any tool you discover that slows or stops the spin cycle is worth having in your survival arsenal.

Believe it or not, one day your journey will end. Thoughts will slow, the pressure cooker will fade from your imagination, and you'll hear the spin cycle only in the washing machine. That's when you know that it really did come to pass.

Yes, there are many things that have to get

done, but in this moment

I have to do nothing.

– Oprah Winfrey

CHAPTER 31

THE MOVE

After countless late nights of trimming, painting, and finishing Mom's new apartment, moving day finally arrived. Mom said "good-bye" to the beloved home she enjoyed with my father and spent the day with a friend while we executed the move.

Our goal was to have her furniture arranged, curtains up, bed made and the picture of my father placed above the dresser where she could see it when she **came home**. The rest of the unpacking would happen as time allowed. With the help of our son from California, the only family member to help with the move, we did it!

The smile and simultaneous tears on my mother's face rewarded us as she explored her new world. Knowing that Mom was safe and seeing her reaction to her new home were all we needed to be sure we had made the right decision. My mother and I, each in our own way, expressed our gratitude that we had persevered through a trying time in our lives. Without faith beyond ourselves, neither of us would have survived.

Adjustments were certain, but with only a few steps between us, I hoped the closeness would allow me to relax and no longer feel that I was inhaling one continuous breath. Perhaps I could begin sleeping again and awaken without a clenched jaw or fists.

A new life for all of us had begun.

It takes hands to build a house, but only

hearts can build a home.

– Author Unknown

REFLECTION

FAITH

Faith is a funny thing. Some people say they have no faith while others profess they couldn't exist for one minute without it. Somehow, we all manage to get from one day to the next, regardless of our belief systems.

One of my siblings has a perspective and belief system that is different from mine. I believe in a higher power that I call God. I believe that God is with me, guiding me and trusting me to complete the job at hand. For her, God does it or audibly instructs her in orderly steps. I don't know that entity. I have yet to see God arrive in person to pack boxes, go to the pharmacy, fix food, attend doctor's appointments, or make endless decisions. Truthfully, I would be frightened if that god showed up.

My belief system has certainly been tested over the years, but I never abandoned it—not even in the most trying times. It became my rock to lean against and my strength when I could no longer move. And sometimes I questioned everything. Why this…? How could that…? When would…? In those uncertain moments, I discovered that faith is bigger than me. Faith is bigger than any of us. It's big enough and strong enough to be questioned and still survive.

When answers arrive, just in the nick of time as someone steps in to assist, just when you desperately need it, you might call them coincidences. Those explanations never worked for me or replaced my faith. My belief system—my faith—gave me peace through the storm, strength in the moment and an ability to continue.

Caregiving will definitely test and refine your faith. It might cause you to explore faith in a whole new way or even rail against your past beliefs. I encourage you to give faith a chance; lean on it and see what happens. And when some overwhelming situation arrives and you have done everything you know to do, just wait, and believe that what you need will show up. Believe that you will be given wisdom to work through the problem. I didn't say that it would evaporate (although it might) or take care of itself. You may still have to supply the leg work, but given a direction, it just might seem easier.

Remember that you are enough to do this job but a little outside help never hurt. I don't know how faith works, but I know it does!

CHAPTER 32

OUR NEW LIFE

July arrived. The pace of the past few months left me feeling at least twenty years older than my actual age. Being thrust into the role of full time caregiver for my parents, losing my dad, deciding where Mom would be safest in addition to planning, building, moving, and selling their house, seemed to erode me a bit more every day. My ability to think, at times, became unsure as my brain shifted into slow motion, leaving me a bit frightened when things didn't make sense. It felt like disembarking from a cruise, stepping on to dry land and swearing that the ocean was still under my feet.

Until the days of caregiving began to accumulate, logic had been my default coping mechanism. If I felt conflicted about something, I simply reasoned my way through the situation and decided what to do. The world around me, so clear most of my life, seemed to be somehow clouded as it was blending into shades of gray. Only my love for my husband, my son, and my mother always remained apparent.

A few part-time caregivers came with my mother to our house. I needed their help, especially at night, but it didn't take long for the revolving door of people to feel intrusive. Before the move

I hadn't had time to think about the impact of losing our newly discovered privacy. My husband and I had been focused only on one goal. Get Mom moved. Adjusting to three people living in our home required patience, something I lacked at times.

I held on to my belief that the brain-fade was a symptom of adapting to a new routine in my home with Mom, and only a temporary expression of the changes in our lives. In spite of my ever present fatigue, I was very glad my mother was with us rather than anywhere else. I wanted to enjoy our time together, but the weariness of constantly managing everything sometimes overshadowed my goal. Slowly, I accepted that our living arrangement was a new **normal** and the adjustments that came with it were simply a part of our new life.

REFLECTION

MORE ADJUSTMENTS?

Just when you think that you've found your rhythm and life is going pretty well, **blam!** I can promise you that it won't be the first, last, or only time that you have to back up and start all over again.

You may have completely changed your life for the benefit of the person you care for or, if you're fortunate, just changed your routine for awhile. An unforeseen event occurs. Routines and life as you knew it go right out the window. Here you are, figuring it out all over again and you just got it under control!

Did you ever go to camp when you were a kid? If you did, you might remember one of the counselors, who needed to deliver information, would begin singing, **"Announcements, announcements, a-now-ownce-ments! A terrible death to die, a terrible death to die. A terrible death to be talked to death. A terrible death to die."** Followed once again by the chorus of **"Announcements!"**

You might as well have some fun and just change it to **"Adjustments!"** It feels like a death, and in a way, it is. You just got your sea legs under you and it's time to adjust again. So, sing with me in your head or out loud.

"Adjustments, adjustments, ad-ju-ust-ments! A terrible death to die, a terrible death to die. A terrible death to be changed to death. A terrible death to die. Adjustments, adjustments, ad-ju-ust-ments!"

As long as you are a part of this thing we call life, you will be making adjustments. The rub comes when you have to make them because another person takes precedence over you. I wish that I could give you some really good news, but instead I have to deliver the truth.

Making adjustments is part of it. You can resist them, hate them, make them grudgingly, or just sing the song and go with the flow. It's your choice.

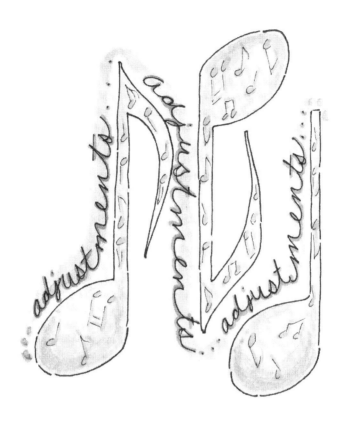

Happiness comes from some curious
adjustments to life.

– Hugh Walpole, Sr.

CHAPTER 33

THE POWER OF THOUGHT

Time marched on. At first, we counted in weeks. Then we counted in months. Eventually, I had to stop and think how long Mom had lived with us. One day I realized that my mother had resided with us for 15 months.

Change became our normal.

My mother slowly deteriorated during those first 15 months as she lost abilities, causing her world to shrink. I tried not to focus on the spiral of her decline, however I could not ignore the gradual progression from a cane and then permanently to a walker, accommodating her advancing neuropathy. Some days our eyes filled with tears about her difficulty in performing simple tasks. Getting bathed and dressed required an exhausting effort for both of us. Being properly dressed was still very important to Mom, so we concentrated on the goal, no matter how long it took.

Mom's mental changes were more subtle than the physical ones. Periodically she awoke **knowing** that her mother was staying with us. Although Mom knew her own chronological age was over 90, she didn't seem to remember her mother dying many years before at the age of 70. Mom even set her breakfast table for two and made extra coffee to serve her mother on more than one occasion. Mom seemed comforted by the thought of her mother being there. And then she would fully awaken and be embarrassed by the thought that my grandmother could not possibly be with her.

Allowing my mother to feel her own feelings, dream her own dreams, and express her own emotions was always important to me. I wanted that time in her life to be as pleasant as possible.

As my mother needed more help, I had a choice to make. I provided the help myself or I bought it. Both options brought anxiety and additional stress with them. I found myself lost in the process of thought, again. If I could get the thinking part straight, the physical somehow showed up. I wondered if I could think money and energy into existence…

Life is not the way it's supposed to be.
It's the way it is. The way you deal with it
is what makes the difference.

– Virginia Satir

REFLECTION

ACCEPTANCE

The person you care for needs help or you wouldn't be assuming this position. Often, an undesirable intimacy evolves between you. No one enjoys having every aspect of their existence observed by another. It's a delicate situation for everyone. You must gather necessary information, while still allowing your patient as much dignity as possible.

In a progressive caregiving situation like aging, you watch and constantly assess the daily changes in mental and physical condition. Observing and evaluating can be an emotional challenge. Don't be surprised if you find yourself retreating behind an imaginary wall where your emotions are less obvious. From that vantage point you can see what is going on without such fervent involvement.

I suggest that you assume the role of watcher. Watch and deal with the situation at hand and move on. Accept what is happening. Accept that today is the day you have. Give thought to the future, but live today. This is where you and your family member live—in this moment. Live here. Make decisions as they are needed and accept that you are enough to do this job of caregiving.

And should a day arrive when you are no longer enough, you will recognize and know that it's time for a new plan. That is part of acceptance, too. I would never mislead you into thinking that what I am saying is easy. It is not easy, but it is possible.

Keep the eyes of a watcher,
stay in the moment, and
live in acceptance.

CHAPTER 34

TEARS

Trying to cling to the threads of my unravelling life, I was falling apart and did not even realize it. Mom's apartment was always spotless, but my house, dusty from lack of attention, waited. I could not remember the last time I vacuumed my own carpet or cleaned the bathrooms.

Eighteen months had passed since Mom moved into her apartment. December began with the grind of the daily routine, compounded by the pressure of Christmas preparations. After more than two years of continuous caregiving, my coping ability had dissolved. I cried so often that my red, swollen face seemed normal. I cried for no apparent reason during commercials, television programs, and minor discussions with my husband. I no longer recognized myself. The stoic girl, once determined to wear contact lenses even if they were the size of bottle caps, was absent. What happened to her? Where did she go?

One morning when helping Mom dress I noticed a strange quarter-sized lesion on the back of her leg. "What could this possibly be? How could we deal with one more thing?" I thought.

"Mom, how long has this thing been on your leg?" I asked.

"What thing?" she queried. "I never noticed anything before. It doesn't hurt!"

It didn't hurt. That was both the blessing and the curse. Mom had been gradually losing feeling in her feet and legs for several years. Even her cat's toy mouse that ended up in her shoe causing her toes to be restricted and the resulting loss of several toenails didn't bother her! Trying to observe Mom's body without making her feel like a science project was an ongoing challenge. Sometimes I cried because of my observations, and other times we laughed until we couldn't stand up. Thankfully we never lost our ability to laugh. Going to the foot doctor because of the disappearing toenails, seeing the expression on his face when he pulled the toy mouse from her shoe and our spontaneous side-splitting laughter was one of those times!

We visited Mom's regular physician because I didn't know what else to do about the lesion. His recommendation regarding the new development was to see a plastic surgeon. My intuition balked, but the obedient child within accepted an appointment his receptionist booked on our behalf.

A week later, we made the trip to the surgeon who, after telling us of his great importance in the world and briefly examining Mom's leg, told his nurse to schedule surgery after the holidays. Turning back to us he said, "With the location and appearance of this type of thing, there's a high probability of malignancy." I felt exhaustion being replaced by panic as I rolled the word **malignant** over and over in my mind. As quickly as the panic appeared, I commanded it to leave. There was no time to deal with that!

When I expressed my concern about caring for Mom after surgery and her difficulty handling anesthesia, I was brushed off as if I knew nothing. Having cared for her after other surgical procedures, I knew that I must plan for the inevitable. Being belittled by DR. IMPORTANCE put the little girl within, in the corner. However, from that corner a still small voice screamed loud enough for me to hear. "This is not right!" But, I didn't know what to do.

I constantly cried about the impending procedure as I contemplated the impact on my mother and me. I could no longer manage without a break, so I contacted *SANCTIMONIOUS SHIRLEY* to see if she could possibly come for a few days in January prior to Mom's surgery. Her reply, "No, but I will come on Saturday."

"What Saturday?" I asked.

"The day after tomorrow," she said.

Her answer brought on a flood of new tears, as if there were any new tears.

I couldn't understand my reaction. I cried because my sister was coming and also because she was not coming at the time I thought I needed her. She seldom came when I requested help, but at least she had visited Mom a few times since the move. That was more than any of my other sisters and relatives did. So, I should have been happy or relieved or something other than just sad and overwhelmed. What had happened to me?

When the tears briefly subsided, I decided we needed a second opinion regarding Mom's leg. My support group of friends provided the resources I needed to find a dermatologist who would accept a new patient. Getting an appointment was only part of the ordeal as the difficulty in taking Mom anywhere was increasing. She walked with ever more effort. Her balance, almost nonexistent, meant a greater physical dependence on me. The challenge to support her, open doors, negotiate elevator doors that closed too quickly, while carrying necessary paperwork that must accompany us everywhere, grew with every appointment. The alternative was hoisting a wheelchair in and out of the car and both Mom and I resisted that as long as possible.

My sister arrived as she planned, in time to help us with the trip to the new doctor. Just to have someone open the doors was remarkably helpful and for that I was grateful.

Thirty minutes after entering the dermatologist's office, the lesion was removed and prepared for analysis. The lab reported **no cancer**. The procedure happened so quickly my mother didn't even have time to worry. My overwhelming relief was replaced by **nurse mode** as I learned about wound care and properly dressing Mom's leg until the site healed over the next twelve weeks. At least there was no hospital stay or general anesthesia to compound everything. When I absorbed the reality of my decision about the doctors, I cried again, but this time with gratitude that my flagging intuition still worked.

A few days later I dragged myself to my own doctor's appointment for a regular check up, six months overdue, where I sobbed the entire time. My blood pressure was dangerously high and I felt like I was spinning apart. My doctor probed, "Have you ever thought of counseling?" "What coping techniques are you using now?" Questions. More questions. I cried without stopping. I was willing to accept any suggestion to stop the tears, even a psychologist.

Counseling sessions were not foreign to me. Many years before I'd worked with a counselor to sort things out, but I'd never before cried through an entire appointment. My first session resulted in a prescription for anti-depressant medication and another appointment a few days later.

I was weak from all the crying and, in spite of SANCTIMONIOUS SHIRLEY'S temporary presence, felt utterly alone in caring for my mother. Although my sister prepared Mom's meals and kept her company, responsibility for every decision still weighed heavily upon me. My sister never wanted to make decisions that might have any possible, future ramification. She did, however, always find the words to chastise me. She strongly suggested, "You would do well to read the Bible more and pray more often. After all, God is the only answer to every problem." I couldn't disagree with her opinion, but never once did God, himself, take my mother to a single doctor's appointment, cut her hair, paint her fingernails her favorite shade of Lisa Pink, bathe her, pay her bills, take her shopping or out to lunch. Nor did He fix her meals, wash her clothes, manage her many medications, or find activities to give her life meaning. When quietly trying to explain my point, SANCTIMONIOUS SHIRLEY'S only response was her typical, "I know," followed by a somewhat pious look, as though I just wasn't enlightened enough to understand.

Since I was not responding to her version of guidance, SANCTIMONIOUS SHIRLEY apparently saw the need to change the subject. She thanked me for letting her come and visit Mom. Of all my sisters, she lived the furthest away and was the only one to spend more than three hours at a time with our mother since we moved Mom to live with us. My attitude softened a bit as I said, "You know, I really appreciate the fact that you came to see Mom. It really has helped."

Before she turned to go back to Mom's apartment, she smiled and said, "You know, coming here is wonderful. It's just like a vacation for me!" In that moment, I realized that the only support I thought I had from family was just a figment of my imagination. My sister had used our situation and my home to escape her own. After that visit, SANCTIMONIOUS SHIRLEY never returned to stay again. Without saying a word, I managed to close her imaginary hotel.

I found myself sitting in the pharmacy parking lot, crying for a whole new host of unidentified reasons. I could not imagine getting out of my car and walking into the store. My cell phone rang as I was trying to find enough energy to move. I could barely say hello.

"Mom, what's going on?" my son asked.

"I can't stop crying... I'm not coping very well... went to my doctor... got sent to a counselor and now they want me to take drugs. Drugs! I can't do that... I gripe all the time about how many prescriptions your grandmother takes..." I managed between bouts of shuddering sobs.

And then my son said something that I will never forget.

"Mom, I'm giving you permission to fill that prescription. It's okay to get some help.

His words gave me courage to leave my car and enter the pharmacy where I filled dozens of prescriptions each year for my mother. This time, the prescription was for me. The pharmacist looked at the paper and then at me. Instantly recognizing the drug's name, she looked at me with more compassion than I had seen in anyone's eyes in months and asked, "Are you okay?" I could only shake my head and try to stop the tears from spilling. Trying not to draw attention to us, the pharmacist quietly nodded and efficiently filled the bottle. As she handed it to me, she said, "Let me know if there is anything I can do to help."

Three days later, my sister returned to her home and my continuous tears stopped as if someone turned a tap. No more sadness. No more anguish. No more overwhelm. Then a strange, new, frightening and almost wonderful realization dawned; I no longer felt anything at all.

There are times in our lives when we are on narrow roads. At those times, we are fools if we try to maintain our usual speed.

– Author Unknown

REFLECTION

RELIEF

Caregiving is stressful; an understatement, to say the least. Coping with a continual state of change and accompanying stress means that you need to formulate a strategy to get relief. You will need it. Seeking relief does not mean you are incapable or somehow lacking. It simply means that you need help.

Give some thought to the following and see if one or more fits your situation:

Search the Internet. An amazing network connects people all over the world. Venting is one of the best uses for online caregiving groups. Just typing your frustrations and hitting **send** may be enough relief to allow patience for another moment, hour, or day. You can find dedicated caregiving support groups for very specific situations. Communicating with people who actually understand your challenges lends validation and connection, perhaps nonexistent in your daily life.

Caregiver support groups are frequently available through local hospitals. The group I attended met monthly. A speaker presented a short program about some aspect of caregiving and I always learned something. Even though I was still dealing with caregiving, I was physically away from the environment and able to make contact with other people who understood the journey. The live group is both a blessing and a challenge. Getting out by yourself feels refreshing, but making and executing the plan to leave may take perseverance. Just do it!

Counseling is a great option. When I knew that I was paying someone to listen to me, I never felt odd about rattling on about my life. With friends I felt that I should edit my speech and always give them time to vent, too. Not only did my counselor listen, she gave me practical ideas to add to my arsenal of coping skills.

Journaling is a great relief for lots of people. Write it down. Close the book and let it go, as best you can. I always warned the people I lived with not to read my journal unless they wanted to get depressed! At first it was only a place to vent my emotions without judgment. As time went by I was able to write about the blessings in my life, a sign to myself that I was making progress. Your writings should fill the purpose that you intend for yourself and no one else.

Visual Journaling may allow you to actually **see** how you feel in a totally different way. I recommend the book ***Visual Journaling, Going Deeper than Words*** by Barbara Ganim and Susan Fox. You do not have to be an artist. You don't even have to be able to draw a straight line! You only have to be open to what you are feeling. And, if you don't know what you are feeling, just start doodling. Visual journaling is an amazing tool to help in the healing process, too.

Medication is an option. I have yet to meet anyone, in person or online, who has been a caregiver more than two years, who has not turned to some sort of anti-depressant help. A plethora of medications are available, so don't settle for one that isn't working for you. There are also alternative **supplements** that may carry fewer side effects than medication. A search engine on the Internet is valuable for researching those possibilities.

If you are lucky enough to have **supportive family** members, tell them what you need and when. Never assume that they will observe or know when to help. And, if you don't have a supportive family, you are not alone. Caregiving duties are guaranteed to reveal chasms in a family if a stress fracture already exists or even create chasms where none existed before, magnified by differences that grow into unbridgeable divides.

Hopefully, you have cultivated a network of **friends** before the season of caregiving finds you. This is one of your greatest options for relief. Friends are part of your life by choice. Some of the best advice my mother ever pounded into my head was, **"to have a friend, you have to be a friend."** I used to hate it when she repeated the same things over and over. I hated it until moments in time always showed me the truth in her words.

Remember to keep your eyes and ears open. Relief may be one magazine article, one television show or one conversation away.

CHAPTER 35

VACATION

Eight months elapsed after the day in the pharmacy parking lot. I chose to name that period my vacation, not because I was away having fun, but because I was actually vacant. I was able to continue caring for my mother, but I experienced no emotion at all, a complete antithesis of my emotional state before the drug. My mother didn't seem to recognize any difference in me as her failing body demanded most of her attention.

I tried not to dwell on the realization that caregiving had overtaken everything in my life. Sometimes it was hard to believe it had only been three years since my parents were hospitalized together. The pride I'd felt in contributing to our finances after all the years devoted to raising the kids dwindled into dejection. My design business now limped along as lack of attention quietly extinguished the income. I had invested myself in the business and then watched it fade away. The antidepressant medication benevolently numbed the loss of my dad, my income, my relationship with my sisters and my self worth.

During the months of swallowing the daily medication, logic was my only tool. Neither intuition nor emotion assisted me. Relationships deteriorated as I grew comfortable in a space void of feeling. It wasn't a bad place. It felt quite peaceful, not having to participate in emotions. Yet somehow from that far away place, I began to miss joy and happiness. The drug not only stopped my tears and depression, it robbed me of any zest for life. I faced another choice, either continuing an existence in my nebulous universe or stopping the drug to reunite with my emotions. I chose the latter.

Withdrawal from the drug was much like returning from a sabbatical. I was not sure that I wanted to come back. Nothing was comfortable for months as the drug leaked from my physical system. Slowly my brain and body reacquainted. Finding my way out of that far-away space required time and patience.

The vacation months remained hazy and I remembered very few details. Counseling sessions continued from time to time as I felt the need. Gradually, my soul again found joy and laughter. The tears were no longer omnipresent. I began to feel. I even began to feel good again.

In time I was glad to have all aspects of my mind and body reunited.

REFLECTION

GOING THROUGH THE MOTIONS

The human body is amazing! It carries on multiple processes without conscious thought. Circulatory, immune, cardiovascular and nervous systems go about their jobs whether you are awake or asleep. Once given food, the digestive system even functions without your help. Some processes, like breathing, carry on without your concentration, but interestingly may be affected when given your attention. I told you it was amazing!

When you contemplate how efficiently the body works without your input, you begin to grasp the idea of your own ability to multi-task while in a state of limited awareness. Habits take over while alertness sleeps for awhile. You literally **do** your life without **feeling** it—motions without minding.

If you find yourself going through the motions and not knowing how you got there, just let go. Remember the kite from **Chapter 26**? Let the kite carry the **not-knowing** away for a moment. Just focus on your breathing. Take big, deep breaths. Hold the breath and then blow it out with a sigh. Sighing is one way the body relieves the stress of fatigue, exhaustion, grief, or sorrow. The more you sigh, the more stress you let go of in that moment.

That's it. Breathe in, Sigh... Let go

Repeat

Breathe in, Sigh.... Let go

When you can, return to awareness.
Return to the moment.
Welcome back!

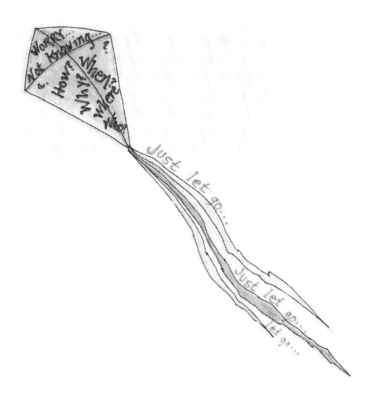

Just let go...

CHAPTER 36

FRIENDS AND FAMILY

Through my counseling appointments and journaling I began to understand more about our family's unwritten code. Our parents raised us to believe that family members were the only people we could count on. I was encouraged to have friends but not to let them take priority over anyone in my family. To compound their myth of the trustworthiness of relatives, my parents also somehow communicated that our family was perfect, and I believed them.

Time has a way of revealing truth.

As the youngest in the family, pleasing, cooperating and obeying became familiar from the moment I was born. I tried very hard not to rock the perfect family boat. Although an unspoken barrier existed between my sisters and me, due to the difference in our ages, I loved my sisters and did my best to help and support them. Only when the fissures in my family became obvious did I begin to question my value in **the boat**.

As the duties associated with caregiving grew, I believed that when I needed my sisters to help with our parents, there would be no hesitation. They were, after all, **our** parents. Stress and responsibilities mounted daily after my father's passing. Although I did not want to acknowledge it, my sisters' lack of value for my mother and me became impossible to ignore. Rarely did family members step in to provide physical or emotional help. Instead, their judgment grew to a crushing proportion as they dissected my decisions and actions from afar. This was the perfect family I believed in?

One day I could no longer ignore the **Truth**. Family is far more than genetics. My real family—my friends—were there all the time. Life experiences were the ties that bound us together through play dates for our children, sharing meals and being available for each other. Together we faced the all-consuming challenge of raising our babies into productive adults and so much more.

As the years passed, several of us found ourselves in unplanned positions of caring for elderly family members. Once again, we shared our experiences, meals, and availability as need and stress levels ebbed and flowed. Family is much more than DNA and a shared last name. It took me quite a while to see the Truth, but with grateful eyes and an open heart I recognized my **real**, amazing family.

A friend is someone who knows the song in
your heart and can sing it back to you when
you have forgotten the words.

– Antonio Porchia

REFLECTION

FRIENDS - GET SOME!

If you find yourself isolated due to broken relationships within your family, you are not alone. See if any of the following statements ring's a bell. If so, know that you are part of the majority of caregivers.

- One person in a family assumes most of the caregiving responsibilities.
- The person who assumes the role of caregiver may become the object of criticism and suspicion, often brought on by others' opinions concerning money.
- One voice from the family group rises.
- The family abandons the caregiver.

So, what is a caregiver to do? First, give up expectations of family members unless you are prepared for disappointment. Instead, invest yourself in cultivating as many quality friendships as you can. This is a key to caregiving survival!

Friends are one of the boundless resources in this life!
Get some!

CHAPTER 37

GUILT?

Questions continually flooded my mind. Two of them fought incessantly for control.

What else could I do to make this situation better? How could I love my mother so much and yet yearn for the day when this part of my life was behind me?

Guilt swept over me as I felt resentful about the disappearance of the line between my mother's life and mine. Why did I feel guilty? Had I done something wrong that would lead me into guilt? The tiny voice from within suddenly grew into an entire chorus. **NO! I would do nothing other than what I have done.**

I tried to understand the answer and yet there were moments when emotion ruled and nagging **what ifs** tempted me. What if I had refused to accept my father's demand to be in charge? What if I had moved my mother into assisted living rather than with us? What if I had been part of a supportive family? What if I didn't feel so weak? If I bit the guilt-bait, the result was always a loop of self-deprecating questions that led me back to second-guessing my decisions.

Contemplating the word, **Guilt**, I remembered reading a book by Wayne Dyer where he suggested that if a shift in behavior was needed, guilt could be a great motivator for change. If my feeling of guilt was real, what did I need to change? Being a full time caregiver had already changed my life, my home, my business, and many relationships. Perhaps the word, **Guilt**, was disguising the real emotion.

An uncomfortable, but persistent thought occurred to me. Maybe what I labeled as guilt was really just **anger**. In the silence between my questions, I had to admit that **anger** had driven me during the past several years... **anger** at my sisters for abandoning me emotionally and physically as I made life-changing decisions for our parents... **anger** that my life had been swallowed up in planning, caring, and executing nearly every detail of my parents' existence while slowly losing control over my own life. I had somehow harnessed the powerful emotion of **anger** and used it as fuel. Sometimes self-analysis is enlightening. Sometimes, it feels awful.

The act of accurately naming the feeling revealed new questions.

Would I continue to let **anger** drive me?
Or, would I choose a different motivator?

I had become so consumed by daily activities that I lost all connection to any motivation beyond mislabeled **anger**. When I remembered that I retained all power to be who I wanted to be, a new decision was possible.

First, I chose to begin the process of recapturing my creativity, my real life-fuel. The freedom of my new decision allowed me to look forward instead of only behind.

Next, I created an imaginary game. I built a box, dumped in an enormous burden of **anger**, closed it up, left it, and walked away, hoping never to use that life-fuel again.

I no longer needed something so powerfully detrimental to empower me. It freed me to walk away from the black box of anger and toward finding myself again.

ℒ ℒ ❦ ℒ ℒ

REFLECTION

FUEL

What keeps you going? What's your fuel?

Take a moment and contemplate your first answer. It's probably the accurate one and may surprise you. Something gives you the drive to keep going, and you need to know what it is. It may have a positive flavor and then again, it may be an emotion like anger, a very powerful motivator.

Why would you even need to know what keeps you in the caregiving arena? To begin with, you have no idea how long this part of your life may continue. Fuel like anger or guilt can exact a powerful toll on your mind and body. Also, don't be surprised if your motivation for caring for someone changes over time. You may begin caregiving with love and compassion, but time and dwindling emotional or physical resources may cause an evolution into resentment or fear.

Your emotions are not good or bad. They are what they are. I'm just encouraging you to take a good look at what puts gas in your tank to get from one day to the next. How do you feel at the end of the day? Do you find yourself wishing that everything was different than it is?

If your answer is, "Are you crazy? Yes, I want things to be different!," it might be time to find a way to take the edge off your stress. Try some deep breathing. The simple act of deep breathing is one of the most positive things you can do for your mind and body. Let the stress that you're holding inside escape as you exhale. As you breathe, be open to the possibility of a new perspective. You may not be able to easily change your situation, but remember that you do have control over your outlook.

A little self-analysis now and then can be very helpful.

Perhaps it's time for a shift in attitude which carries over into your fuel of choice. It's never too late to make a new decision.

CHAPTER 38

WATCHING AND WAITING

A new day arrived bringing with it my fresh determination to accomplish things. I made a list. Top priority included long-neglected responsibilities of dusting, cleaning bathrooms and vacuuming floors. First, the mundane. I wanted those tasks finished quickly and efficiently, with a sense of completion, so I could focus on the important part of my list, the soul-food of creating something—drawing, sewing, painting—anything.

In a split second, everything changed. Something was wrong with Mom. I didn't know what **it** was. Her speech was normal, but her comprehension was absent. She seemed to hear me as I spoke, but her responses were odd and her body movements more awkward than usual.

So, the waiting began—again. The paralysis of waiting and watching, an all too familiar state, settled around me.

Instead of marching through my list, the bathrooms and carpet stayed untouched as watching replaced work. I looked for any changes that might signal a need for something. When Mom dropped off to sleep in her much loved lift-chair, I watched to see if her chest continued to rise and fall.

I waited as a merry-go-round of new questions circled inside my head. "Should I call the doctor? What can the doctor do? More tests? More medicine? Time in a hospital? How badly would she be affected by a hospital stay? What abilities would she lose this time? Could I handle the situation if she did not go to the hospital? How much longer could this possibly go on?" On and on the questions spun—sometimes at the speed of light and in the blink of an eye, everything dragged to a halt.

Like so many other days, I watched and waited again, nearly paralyzed.

My husband helped me design and plant flower gardens around our house. Some of the gardens were well established, but we created others just for my mother. By spending a few minutes in the gardens, I discovered a way to cope with the waiting. I added new colors and textures to the beds and anticipated the rainbow of blooms. Not only did our little park help me, it also entertained my mother. On good days, I helped her walk through the gardens where, depending on the season, we admired and talked about the daffodils, columbine, Hibiscus, Hostas, lilies and roses. Mom often smiled as she remarked that my father would have been proud of my work. When walking was too difficult, Mom watched from her bay window or sat in a chair on the deck. The gardens gave us both a temporary escape from our reality.

Books filled more of the waiting. My earliest memory of books is as a preschooler lying on a bed, feeling the coolness of my great-aunt's beautiful Sunbonnet Baby quilt on my legs, surrounded by a pile of little Golden books. The same characters marched around the border of each book and I studied them every afternoon before "reading" the story until I fell asleep. As I grew up, my love of books never waned. When I needed an escape from life, I chose a novel to read—a good story or something cheesy. When I wanted to learn things, I turned to my ever growing library of nonfiction. My books never let me down.

My mother still liked to read when her unpredictable eyes could focus. She loved a good plot and a happy ending, as did I. I guess we both found comfort in an imaginary world created by our books when time no longer mattered and the paralysis of waiting evaporated for a while.

At some point, I realized that my mother was waiting, too.

Moving beyond the state of paralysis required a decision. The longer the caregiving lasted, the less energy I had for anything beyond the imperative. My life goals shifted from building my business to hoping I could keep it alive. I no longer expected to have the taxes filed on time. I just hoped I could beat the second extension. I gave up the expectation of a tidy house and just tried to keep the dishes washed. I attempted to keep up with the laundry, but even that was difficult. Somehow, I had to find a way through the waiting.

Being paralyzed is a lot like being overwhelmed. Both states have the same outcome; nothing gets done. By lowering my expectations, I could make a list of intentions, but not the list with which I began the day. Instead of doing all the laundry, I could do one load. Instead of cleaning the kitchen, I could unload the dishwasher. Instead of cleaning all the bathrooms, I could clean a sink. Instead of drawing for an hour, I could dash out a quick sketch or leaf through one of my art books. Each item on my new list, when completed, left behind a small sense of accomplishment, an antidote to being overwhelmed and paralyzed.

When unexpected moments appeared and Mom felt energetic enough to go out for lunch or just out on the deck for a cup of coffee, I grabbed them. In time, these tiny vacations from the waiting disappeared, too. Somehow, instinctively I captured those vignettes, realizing that clean bathrooms and dust-free furniture could never replace my memories.

As another day came to a close with the usual mental and physical fatigue, Mom appeared to have settled back into being comfortable. My childhood habit of trying to relax by reading led me to one of my favorite books where I happened across the following quote from Anthony Robbins, a motivational speaker and writer.

"God's wealth is circulating in my life. His wealth flows to me in avalanches of abundance."

I was reminded once again by those words that wealth is far more than money. Wealth circulates within experiences and memories and relationships. By slowing down, sometimes to the point of paralysis, I redefined my life. I realized that life comes in seasons. This part of my life was just a season. There would be other seasons for creating and building. The season that I so often named **paralysis**, I renamed **stillness**. This season, too, was filled with riches and a new label gave me the power to embrace them.

No longer did I allow the stillness of watching and waiting stop my life. Instead, with gratitude I lived the moments of the season and savored the riches of memories-in-the-making as they circulated in my life.

ॐ ॐ ॐ ॐ ॐ

Gratitude is when memory is stored in the heart and not in the mind.

– Lionel Hampton

REFLECTION

BEAUTY

When you are overtaken by responsibilities, it is so easy to miss the good stuff! This can happen especially when you are dealing with the details of someone else's life.

The reality of caregiving is, that even with a specific diagnosis, you have no idea how long you will be needed as the caregiver. It begins benignly enough in lots of situations. You think that it will only last a short time, and then you can get back to your own life.

When I faced the fact that my parents needed help, it was October. Someone mentioned the word January to me and in utter disbelief I said, "There's no way I can do this until January!" However, in reality my active caregiving days lasted for several years.

After the initial shock of becoming a caregiver lessens a bit, you will need to find ways to cope. I keep beating this drum, but it's the absolute truth with a **capital T**. Life can become shades of gray as stress accumulates, masking the beauty surrounding you. I won't kid you into thinking that it's a breeze to switch back into living color, as the old television slogan said. But, if you fail to see beauty around you, you will wake up one day and wonder where all the time went.

Find ways to take mini-vacations, through reading a book or listening to it on your iPod. (By the way, if you don't have an iPod or something like it, get one!) Plant some flowers. Even one single pot of flowers can remind you of growth and the beautiful things in life.

Use your imagination. Take note and participate in the beauty all around while you are a caregiver.

Everything has beauty,

but not everyone sees it.

– Confucius

CHAPTER 39

RESPITE

I was told by authorities in the health care field that any caregiver must have Respite in order to continually care for someone. In fact, they are adamant about the need for Respite. Interestingly, no one seemed to be able to tell me what it meant or how to get it. And, by the time I used my energy dealing with any given day's events, I had none left to figure it out.

According to **The American Heritage Dictionary of the English Language**, Respite is defined as a temporary cessation or postponement; usually of something disagreeable.

What a distasteful way to describe my need! On top of being tired beyond description, stressed to the point of breaking,

Respite tempora
cessation or
postponement, usu
something disagre
a break.

I had to find a way to get a temporary postponement from a disagreeable situation. I never considered caring for my mother to be a disagreeable situation—difficult, yes—disagreeable, no! So, I added confusion to the pile of thoughts that I had to sort out—when I found time.

A break—that's what I chose to call my need for Respite. Experience taught me that I did not really relax unless a break lasted for more than a few days. During the past several years, I had taken rare, short vacation trips, so I knew the sizable preparations to be made in order for me to be gone. I needed to hire additional caregivers to replace me, not to mention the people to prepare and serve meals. Any appointments that occurred while I was gone necessitated a driver and then I had to find someone trustworthy enough to handle the finances. Medications had to be organized along with emergency plans. It seemed like all I did was make lists and more lists.

The resources required for making so many preparations were absent, yet I absolutely needed a break. In a nebulous place just before waking, where I sometimes solved problems, a possibility arrived. I wondered if any of the local assisted living facilities offered short term stays for someone in our situation. I decided to ask. After a few phone calls, I scheduled a couple of appointments to explore our options.

One facility looked promising and the administrator understood my need for a break from the responsibilities of caregiving. She arranged a tour for my mother and me, hoping that when the time arrived for Mom to stay, things would have a bit of a familiar feel. My mother thoroughly enjoyed seeing the facility and even recognized several acquaintances who lived there.

I planned the respite visit for a three-week period, allowing me a chance to really relax. A lot of time and effort went into the temporary move, but it was totally worth it! My mother survived very well, and I rested for the first time in several years. The change of scenery was good for my mother, and the lack of routine re-energized me. Even a day of moving Mom and her possessions back home could not exhaust me.

The break in my daily life began to illuminate the meaning of the phrase "caregivers must take care of themselves first." I had read it, heard it, contemplated it, yet never really understood how to take care of myself first. I realized that respite was not a cessation of something disagreeable. It was actually refreshing and positive for both Mom and me.

REFLECTION

GET HELP

O nce, in casual conversation, a very good friend threw me a lifeline. She said, "Make a decision. It is the right one for the moment." Such a simple statement carries a lot of power.

When you realize that you need a break from caregiving, pay attention. It's time to get help in some form. If you are lucky enough to have supportive relatives, ask them for help. You might take your family member to them or have them physically relieve you so you can take a vacation. Another idea is for your patient to visit a friend, so you can stay home without having to be a caregiver at all for a period of time. That can feel like a wonderful vacation. If family or friends are not available, check into assisted living facilities for a temporary stay. In-home caregiving businesses are becoming more readily available so check them out, too.

- The first step toward a much needed break is the realization that you need it.
- The second is making the necessary arrangements.
- The third step is enacting the plan.

Do not second-guess your decision. Rest in knowing that you have made the best decision for the moment. Do not waste your valuable respite time with fret and worry. Instead, spend your time playing and enjoying yourself.

Respite means taking a refreshing break from the everyday routine. Respite means the caregiver must do self-care in order to take care of anyone else. You really need to plan for respite and if you can't imagine how to accomplish getting a break, do the following:

- **ASK**. Ask questions. Make phone calls. Look for agencies or businesses who specialize in supplying help. Keep asking until you find someone to give you respite.
- **ACT** on the answer. Make a plan. Select a date.
- **REST** and know that the decision you make at the time is the right one.

My friend threw me the lifeline, and now I throw it to you. "Make a decision. It is the right one for the moment."

There is nothing to be gained by waiting for a better situation. You see where you are and you do what you can with that.

– Jacob K. Javits

CHAPTER 40

A NEW DECISION

After my mother's three week stay at the assisted living facility, she returned home feeling positive about her experience, yet very glad to be back in her apartment.

A few short weeks later, Mom's body suddenly declined and the pressure of caring for her ramped up dramatically. She experienced increasingly frequent periods when her awareness dimmed and even more imaginary people visited her. There were additional physical demands on my body as her care became more intense as well as an undeniable truth about the dwindling financial resources. The non-medical caregivers who helped my mother several hours weekly could no longer help Mom with some of her daily activities because of her growing instability. They still provided valuable companionship, but everything involved with caring for her rested with me.

Some days Mom's legs were so unpredictable that the simplest tasks she normally performed were nearly impossible. Everything stacked up to a towering house of cards. I felt the old wellspring of tears bubbling up again.

I wanted Mom to remain with us as long as she could. Our original plan was for her to live with us until her last day on this earth. As the months had become years, I could no longer deny the truth. I was completely worn out, and I had no ability to pay more people to replace me. My mother was in need of additional supervision and help that, I had to admit, I could not provide. Long ago I promised my mother that I would never move her to a facility unless she was no longer cognizant. Hindsight—always so sharp—taught me that making promises I might not be able to keep, was ill-advised.

I loved my mother so much.

I no longer possessed the ability to care for her at home. Such an admission carried with it crushing defeat. Loving my mother and knowing what I had to do magnified everything in our lives. I had to make my decision based solely on what was best for her. I struggled to reconcile my mind and my heart. The desires of my heart were so clear, but reality could no longer be ignored. What were we to do?

We had to make a change – a new decision.

After scrutinizing her finances and facing Mom's needs, I accepted that the best choice for my mother was a permanent move to an assisted living facility. There, she would have 24 hour help and constant medical supervision.

The time arrived for me to talk to my mother about the move, as long ago I agreed never to keep secrets from her. One morning while we sat on her deck with piping hot cups of coffee, I said, "Mom, we need to talk."

"Okay," she said with some hesitation.

"You are needing more help now. I just can't do everything the way I've been able to for the past several years."

"I know. It's not fair to you," she said.

"Well, Mom, it's not about being fair. It's about your safety and having help when you need it."

Tears began trickling down our cheeks at exactly the same moment.

"What are we going to do?" she asked.

"I think that a move to the assisted living facility is the best plan."

Sitting on the deck in silence, we cried. Even though I could reach her by car in just a few minutes, it wasn't the same as being a few steps away. It felt like an eternity passed as we sat together, trying to take it all in. Drying her tears, Mom sat up a bit straighter, took a deep breath and said, "This is what we need to do. I'll be okay. Make the arrangements." Moments passed and slowly we began talking and imagining what life might be like after another move.

I called the facility to finalize our plan only to be given the news that the building was completely full and there was no room for my mother. After the pain of arriving at our decision, we had to wait. We waited for weeks, but in the end, the waiting was a very good thing. The extra time allowed my mother to enjoy all of the summer flowers and lots of time on the deck for coffee in the mornings and barbecue in the evenings. We talked and remembered, and I recorded each memory. Most of the time we ignored the subject of the move, but that was like trying to ignore a massive gray elephant standing in the middle of the room!

We simply kept making memories.

The day arrived when Mom was finally assigned a room. A treasured friend volunteered to help me move my mother's belongings. She understood my emotions, as well as my mother's, because she had also made the same difficult choice for a family member. Having anyone help, especially someone who cared about both of us, gave me the strength to do what had to be done as sadness and failure filled my heart. I refused to give in to the rising river of tears. If the emotional dam began to leak, I did not have the ability to stop the torrent that was sure to follow. My heart was breaking, but I had to ignore it.

Mom and I slowly walked to her new room. I repeatedly assured her that she was staying at the facility but her home was still with us in her apartment. I needed to believe that my words helped her feel less deposited. She nodded silently as we walked down the hallway. After I arranged her room, talked with the nurses and filled out endless forms, the time arrived for me to go home without Mom. Holding back the tears was impossible as I said, "Good bye," to my mother. She tried to be brave, too, but neither of us succeeded. I knew in my heart that I was doing the only thing—the right thing—the best thing for my mother.

As I walked to my car, my feet felt like they were shod in lead. And so did my heart. The heaviness in my heart was called failure. I had made a plan almost four years before that I could not complete. I wondered if I could ever forgive myself. Time would be my healer or my executioner.

REFLECTION

FLEXIBILITY

Well, here you are. You have done your absolute best, and it's not good enough. Now what? This is when flexibility becomes your new tool. Speaking from experience I can tell you that you must remain flexible in your thinking and planning. In spite of gathering information, making a well-informed decision, life can take an unexpected turn and you find yourself back at square one.

Guess what? This may be the best place to be. When you have no idea what to do next or where to turn, you have a choice — become pliable or break under the weight of your choices. Look around. Talk to people. Ask questions. Make new lists.

And you know what else? You may have to do this more than once. Keep your eyes wide open and please listen to me.

Being flexible is key to surviving during your caregiving journey. Admitting that you need help allows possibilities you might never have considered.

CHAPTER 41

ADJUSTMENTS

In some ways, my mother coped with her move to assisted living better than I did. The nurses and staff remembered Mom from her respite visit and made every effort to help her feel comfortable. Mom adapted well to the schedule and in the words of the administrator, "rose to the occasion." I spent time with my mother most every day to make sure that she was well cared for. I needed to know that I could trust the staff to take care of my precious mom.

After the move, Mom enjoyed several calm months. Very few things bothered her. She enjoyed meeting new people and forming relationships with her new caregivers. For me, those months were filled with adjustments. Depression, ever looming, waited for an opportunity to take over. I finally had time to do all the things that I had let go for so long, but I struggled to find any motivation to begin.

Ever so slowly I noticed the constant stress and strain of active caregiving fading as I felt the urge to be creative once again.

Occasionally, I blew the dust from my art supplies and piles of fabrics and began to get reacquainted with them. One step at a time... one day at a time I began trying to redesign my life. With positive physical, mental and emotional changes, I started setting new goals. No longer was I focused solely on maintaining strength and damage control.

I realized that I could finally pay attention to my nutritional needs. Instead of grabbing snacks and quick meals, I read cook books and magazines, educating myself about what my body needed. Adding lots of fresh vegetables and fruits, quality proteins and fats into my diet along with the best vitamin supplements I could find, improved my mental and physical state. As my brain was better nourished, my thinking cleared and I realized that I no longer needed to manage every detail of my mother's life as well as my own. The nagging black dog of depression reared his ugly head less and less. Every day was filled with adjusting to a new life.

**A new realization dawned.
I was once again my mother's daughter.**

I had been in the caregiving role for so long that I had forgotten what it felt like to be a daughter. I could once again spend time with my mother—talking and laughing and even crying, sometimes. We could go to our favorite places for lunch when Mom was strong enough. And as long as she was physically able, I brought her home to her apartment every week where her cat, adjusting to a new dependence on me, was happy to climb onto her lap. Our time together at home was always pleasant as we were mother and daughter once more.

As my brain was better nourished, my
thinking cleared. I realized I was once again
my mother's daughter.

REFLECTION

EMBRACE WHAT IS

One sure thing in life is that everything changes. Isn't that an oxymoron?

If you parented a small child, I'm sure you remember that just when you figured out how to deal with him and what to expect, a **new** child moved in and you started all over with new routines, ways to discipline, and new rewards. That small child has to change, test his boundaries, and try new things in order to grow. It's part of the process, yet the challenged parent often feels resistant, wanting the child to hurry up and get over a given stage so life can be okay again.

Resistance is a common reaction to change. We want to get back to what is comfortable. It's not wrong, but it leads straight to frustration.

Caregiving for the elderly shares many similarities with raising children, but usually in reverse order. Instead of boundaries being tested, the world becomes smaller. Instead of trying new things, the person you care for may flatly refuse to do something he did with ease the day before.

Just when you think you have working systems in place,

something changes and you find yourself having to make adjustments. If you are in a position of caregiving very long, you will be faced with many changes as your patient's abilities diminish. Then comes resistance. Then comes frustration. Something else changes and the cycle repeats again and again and again.

The secret to keeping your sanity during the changes is very simple. Just embrace what is. That's it. Embrace what is. Give up wishing things were some other way than they are. They're not. Resisting the current situation will drive you crazy and intensify every emotion. Whether you want to admit it or not, you have very little power over anything. But, you do have the power to embrace what is.

Deal with whatever you have to deal with—in the moment. Let tomorrow or next week or next month show up. In time, everything will change again and your best plans and preparations will probably go down the drain.

Trying to plan ahead or making contingency plans might work, but usually doesn't. Resisting and wishing things were different is fruitless.

Just remember
Stay in the moment and embrace what is.

CHAPTER 42

EVERYTHING CHANGED

Another July arrived. My mother had lived at the assisted living facility for ten months. They proved to be ten positive months filled with activities, new friendships and a nightly children's card game called Skip Bo. Mom said it was fun because, "You only have to count to twelve!"

I loved watching my mother with her new peer group. I watched as relationships like the one with her much younger "next door neighbor" became important. They watched out for each other and sat at the same table for their meals unless the neighbor was hospitalized. During those days, Mom spent her time worrying about when or if the hospital stay might end and her friend would return. Mothering her friend provided a renewed purpose for Mom's life, enhancing an experience she completely embraced.

As I observed my mother I was surprised when I realized that the pressure for me to be everything to her no longer existed. Often Mom told me, "I really am very happy here. Oh, the food could be a little better sometimes, but if that's all I have to complain about, I have no problems. And as long as I still get to be with you, I'm very happy." Every time I heard her words, I felt the pressure of all the decision making from the past several years release a bit more. My shoulders relaxed. My breathing deepened and I even occasionally slept through the night. While Mom was safely being cared for, I spent the summer tending the flower gardens and adjusting to my new definition of caregiver. Being an overseer rather than actively participating in every aspect of my mother's care was entirely new for me. The touchstone of the earth and the plants helped fill the void I felt because Mom no longer lived with me.

Each month brought about physical and mental changes in Mom as the aging process marched on. Spending time with her was usually pleasant with only an occasional problem to resolve. I made an effort during each visit to express my sincere gratitude to the staff who tenderly cared for her, doing the job I was no longer able to do.

I still managed the shrinking finances, hoping for a miracle that would somehow multiply the money that would be gone

in a matter of weeks. I thought back to the first month that Mom lived in her room at the assisted living facility. Very soon after her move, I wrote a letter to each member of my family explaining why Mom needed round the clock supervision. I enclosed a list of Mom's expenses that would not be covered by her income, hoping that the family would finally step up and help. My eldest sister and her daughter each sent a small amount of money every month. Although I was deeply appreciative, their total contribution wasn't even enough to pay for one month of care. Three other family members decided to pitch in and have a telephone installed in Mom's room and were more than annoyed with my lack of gratitude at their generosity.

I don't know why I ever thought the family dynamics would change.

Family involvement with Mom was limited, by their own choices, to occasional phone calls, letters, and rare visits. Somehow sensing Mom's diminishing mental capacity and vulnerability, my sister no longer needed to wear the mask of EXHAUSTED TERESA. Her real personality—THE EXQUISITE TORTURER—emerged for good. This daughter, author of many hurtful letters and responsible for a lifetime of Mom's heartache, seized yet another opportunity to wound my mother.

One Sunday evening THE EXQUISITE TORTURER phoned my mother and harangued her with **a long, loud, litany of opinions**. She jumped at my mother's child-like willingness to listen as she ranted about me and my highly questionable motives. My mother's ability to comprehend accusation and innuendo was limited. In her heart, Mom knew the truth, but she no longer possessed the capacity to defend her knowledge. Instead, she internalized her anxiety. Her security had been threatened because a seed of doubt, no matter how tiny, had been planted.

The morning after THE EXQUISITE TORTURER'S phone call, a nurse from the assisted living facility called me to report that my mother was bleeding, requiring another trip to the hospital. Suddenly, I retreated from my newly discovered freedom and resumed the all too familiar role of decision maker and active caregiver.

This time, however, my intuition nagged me. It correctly foretold of the enormous impact my decisions would carry for both Mom and me.

The emergency room visit resulted in new doctors who wanted to begin immediate diagnostic testing that frightened and confused my mother. She turned to me for reassurance that I was in charge. The weight of making decisions settled over me like a thick, immobilizing army blanket. After several conferences I determined that invasive testing should wait so we could see if my mother's body might resolve the crisis. Several hours later,

Mom was settled somewhat comfortably in a hospital room that would be her home for the following few weeks.

During those weeks I spent most of my waking hours with her, being her daughter and advocate. Mom often wanted to talk about her inevitable passing, an event she was anticipating with a great deal of anxiety. We spent hours talking and crying and waiting. Time passed at a snail's pace, but Mom and I managed to find things to laugh about, easing some of the tension and uncertainty.

As we waited to see if her body could survive another crisis, I read a book aloud to Mom. It helped to pass the time and took us both to a new place with new imaginary friends. Mom loved hearing a good story and reminded me again how much I loved hearing her read to me when I was a little girl.

Memories. I continued recording each one.

During the hospital episode, Mom insisted that she did not want the rest of her family to visit while she was in the hospital. She was clearly struggling with too many issues to deal with their drama, and although Mom didn't understand all of THE EXQUISITE TORTURER's words during her phone call, Mom remembered how the words made her feel. Mom had no desire to be trapped in a hospital room with her or any of the others. Repeatedly, she told me that she wanted only my husband and me to be with her.

Out of respect for her, I gave SANCTIMONIOUS SHIRLEY Mom's message and asked that she tell the others. In spite of hearing from SHIRLEY, two days later THE EXQUISITE TORTURER issued an edict to the family that it was time to panic and the bulk of them arrived as a group, blatantly refusing to honor my mother's request.

In past rare moments I witnessed my mother rise from within, watched her purse her lips and everyone knew it was time to take the medicine she was ready to dish out. Much to the surprise of the family, their visit proved to be one of those moments.

Mom refused to make eye contact or speak a word to THE

Exquisite Torturer. Mom's silence was as hurtful as her words could be. As other family members spent a bit of private time with her, Mom seized each opportunity to state her opinion of their actions and disrespect. No one expected her to have the ability or the words as she turned the table on them. The visit was not at all as they assumed it would be. In spite of Mom's failing body, for a few moments, her mind and tongue remained sharp.

After receiving Mom's proper shellacking, *The Exquisite Torturer*, along with the others exited, en masse, just as they had arrived.

As the weeks in the hospital crawled by, I wondered how long my mother would survive. She expressed many times during those weeks that she was tired of living and felt that she had lived too long. Even though I tried valiantly to keep my attitude and our conversations positive, Mom's view of her life now amounted to one struggle after another. We shared many more conversations and tears as she finally expressed her one concern—**leaving me**. Holding her hand with tears streaming down my cheeks, I assured my sweet mom that although I would miss her and all the wonderful experiences that we enjoyed together, I would be all right. I told her that when life grew too difficult, I wanted her to let go.

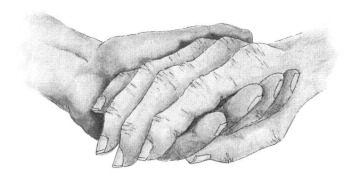

Then, she began leaving a bit at a time.

Mom seemed to be torn between staying and leaving. Sometimes her mind could not seem to hold on to the details of where she was and what was happening. Then just as suddenly as the confusion had settled around her, it lifted and clarity returned. I continued spending as much time as possible with my mother—listening, talking, hoping for some miracle that would make everything okay again until a conversation with the care-coordinator forced me to face reality. Mom had stabilized enough to be released from the hospital, and once again I had to decide what was to happen.

I didn't like being inside my own skin. I didn't want to wrestle with decisions any longer. I was so tired of trying to figure things out, and once again, a monumental decision towered over me. I prayed that neither physical nor mental exhaustion would obscure my thinking.

Mom could not return to the assisted living facility because of her lack of mobility and staggering weakness from being bedridden for several weeks. I envisioned no way to bring her back home because I did not have financial resources to buy assistance. The only option I saw, at the time, was a nursing home because Medicare and her insurance provided help. I was given two days to figure out all the details and try to explain to my mother what was happening.

The nursing home I selected was close to my home, but proximity was its only asset. They were short staffed, residents were unhappy, and it smelled like an old shack. In two days, I realized that I had made an awful decision and I had to do something different. I could not leave my mother in such a pathetic situation. Over and over she said that she just wanted to **go home**. After discussions with people in my support system regarding Mom's fragile condition and exploring every option available to us, I made another choice.

I moved Mom back **home** with a referral to Hospice from her doctor. My husband seriously questioned my decision as he could not imagine us being able to care for Mom by ourselves, but I felt it was my only option. Seeing her face as I gave her the news that she was **going home** was enough to carry me through the next few excruciating weeks. I truly believed that when Mom was at home in her apartment, she would be calm again.

After the move, new people from Hospice had to be oriented and an entirely new routine established. Hospital equipment arrived and transformed my mother's living room. I was given information to read and papers to sign, and almost immediately my body began to show signs of the monumental stress load.

The caregiving journey became a marathon. Interruptions from multiple alarms to check on Mom at night never allowed for a long period of rest. Recognizing the end of one day and the beginning of the next was impossible. Mom's world shrank to a hospital bed, her lift-chair, a wheelchair and a bedside commode. Moving her from one place to another required strength beyond what I had gained during my months of exercise with a personal trainer at the gym. The effort needed to manage Mom's care was beginning to exceed my ability.

The Hospice nurse and social worker encouraged me to welcome each day without unrealistic expectations. I read the information from the Hospice organization and decided that keeping Mom as comfortable as possible was the goal. I was willing to try anything to help my mom as she seemed to be facing the last part of her life. She preferred being in bed much of the time, which necessitated a special air mattress with a dimpled surface, and frequently moving Mom from one position to another to prevent the possible formation of bed sores. Although she appeared to be resting comfortably, it was a constant challenge to keep Mom from slipping toward the foot, which meant figuring out how to repeatedly pull her up without hurting either of us. Sometimes just fluffing her pillow or changing the blanket was enough to put a contented smile on my mom's face.

I wanted the time that Mom had left with us to be as pleasant as possible. Constantly thinking about how I could create a better environment, I remembered how she loved music. I played soft instrumental classics and recordings from my old piano recitals for her. The pleasant expression on her face told me how much she liked listening as she seemed lost in her inner space most of the time. Watching Mom, I could see that her struggle over whether to stay or leave was growing.

In the few free moments while Mom slept, I connected with a support group through my computer. One of them made a passing comment about the soothing nature of an aquarium for elderly people. Knowing that I could not possibly handle the hours needed for keeping an aquarium, I wished for a way to bring something like it into my mother's life. A few days later while picking up some groceries, I noticed a stack of aquarium lamps sitting by the checkout counter. There was nothing real about it, but I thought it was worth a try. The lamp was actually created from rotating fish-embossed paper. As the paper wound slowly around the night-light bulb, the fish appeared to be swimming on the wall. Mom loved them and even thought they were real. One evening I asked Mom if she would like to eat some supper and she responded, "Yes, I really should be getting home now. I need to do something because I sure am tired of fishing!"

Trying to keep my mother somewhat anchored, I placed the photograph of my father where she could see it when she was awake. Beside it, I hung a picture of my son, the one person she had consistently recognized whether in person or on the phone. As I was changing her bed one day, I asked her about the pictures. She thought a moment and said, "Oh, that's my grandson, isn't it?"

"What about the other picture?" I asked, pointing to my dad.

Rather blankly Mom looked at me and responded, "Did I know him?" She continued, "I think maybe I knew him once."

And that's when I knew things were going seriously awry in

my mother's mind. I kept my attention focused on changing her bed and tidying up so as not to register shock on my face as I said, "Oh, that's my dad. Do you remember him?"

"Hmmm. Maybe a little," she said.

And then with a little lilt in her voice she asked, "Is is time for me to go home yet?"

"Mom, this is your apartment. You live with us here. This is your home, right here with me."

"I do? I guess I forgot," she said.

Then the confusion lifted and Mom was back with me for a bit until her next nap, when the cycle of wanting to go home would repeat when she awoke. Mom continued mentally popping in and out during our conversations and I never knew to whom I would be talking. Often she acknowledged another person in the room with us; usually her mother. Sometimes Mom acted as if she didn't recognize herself or me, referring to herself as *she* rather than *I*, almost as if she had stepped away from her body. Then, she forgot where she was again and she wanted to **go home**. My heart and body were breaking. More than ever before, I tried to stay in the moment.

After several weeks, caring for my mother was consuming all of my stamina. I had no idea how long I could hold on, but I became acutely aware that I had assumed a role that would end in defeat. In spite of brief moments when Mom was lucid and clear, she had little understanding of what was happening. Everything was about the present instant and often that was mass confusion.

Her physical comfort was quickly going beyond what I could provide, in spite of my best efforts. As Mom declined, so did I. Her body vacillated from one extreme to the other as systems began to fail. My lack of sleep and appetite sapped my strength. Every muscle in my body began to ache and then spasm. My greatest fear about caring for Mom seemed to be coming true. By losing my health, I knew I could not take care of her. I was not a nurse and had limited access to the overworked Hospice nurses, further illuminating my inadequacy in dealing with Mom's physical issues.

And then came the time for yet another decision.

How could I do this again? How could I make another decision? Just before I moved my mother back into her apartment, in a moment when her mind was focused and clear, she made me and my husband promise that if the situation became too much for me to handle I would do whatever had to be done to care for her and for myself. Weeks without real sleep, limited food, and an ailing body made the decision only slightly easier for me.

A bed opened at one of the best nursing homes in the area. It was a small family-like atmosphere where the staff genuinely cared for the residents. By the time I could get someone to stay with my mother so that I could go visit the prospective home, my body was ill. I could barely speak or hold up my own head, yet I still had to continue. There was no other choice, no help and absolutely no family in sight. Another move meant more papers to sign, plans to make, and information to gather. I was so tired of gathering and providing information; I really did not know if I could do it one more time.

The morning of the move, my mother was lost in her thoughts. Like many other mornings, she did not seem to recognize food or her medication. All she wanted to do was go back to bed. So, while she slept, my husband and I packed the car. At 11:30 a.m., suddenly my mother awoke and she was really my mother! She smiled as I dressed her and explained where we were going. For the first time in weeks Mom announced that she was hungry. I made her favorite peanut butter and jelly sandwich and cut it into triangles, just like I remembered her doing for me when I was a little girl.

Together, my husband and I managed to get Mom into the front seat of the car and settled her with the tiny triangular sandwiches and her favorite protein drink. My husband sat quietly in the back seat, observing the interaction between Mom and me. Between bites, as I drove to the new home, Mom read me the road signs and happily chatted away. When we arrived at the new place, Mom took one look and announced, "This looks like a very nice place and I just know I will like it here!" I was stunned at the unfolding of the day! My mom was herself and happy about everything! I was so glad that my husband was with me. I don't think he could have believed my mom's reappearance without seeing it for himself.

I settled Mom into her room with a new roommate, made her bed with her bedsore-preventing mattress, and then I introduced myself to the new staff. Mom's new surroundings were small, but clean, bright, airy, and fresh. The trip had tired both Mom and me. I still had more legal details to deal with, so I helped Mom into her bed and kissed her forehead. Each time I tucked my mother in bed and said, "Good bye," we knew that it could be the last time we saw each other. One day, that would be reality. I just never knew when.

Before I could fall apart I had to take care of the rest of the paperwork. I retreated behind the uncomfortable, yet familiar fog where life looked very far away. I had visited this space so many times that I was no longer frightened to see it again. My husband patiently waited as I finalized Mom's admission.

Leaving Mom this time was different and my heart knew it. As we left the nursing home, my husband drove the car allowing me to collapse as sobs twisted my body and soul. I could not absorb what I had just done.

I needed my mother's arms to hold me and her lap to fall into. I needed Mom to reassure me that I had done my best. Instead, I felt utter failure, again. Years before, in a conversation with my dad, I had promised him that I would always care for my mother. Admitting that I had made a promise I could not fulfill crushed what was left of my self-worth. I felt as though I had failed myself and everyone else.

I was too tired to think about one more thing. Everything in my body ached but nothing hurt as much as my heart. Failure is a very physical thing.

"Whatever course you decide upon, there is always someone to tell you that you are wrong. There are always difficulties arising which tempt you to believe that your critics are right. To map out a course of action and follow it to an end...

requires courage."

– Ralph Waldo Emerson

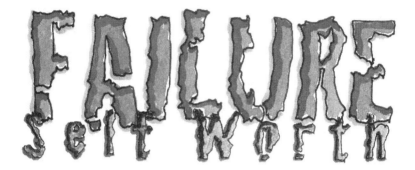

REFLECTION

HARD CHOICES

How I wish I could tell you that your choices as a caregiver would always be positive and well received. I would like to tell you that if your heart is in the right place and you make decisions with love as your motivating factor, the choice you make will be the best and will have a wonderful outcome. I would like to tell you that if you just work at the choice long enough, you'll always feel good about it. I owe you more than that.

Here's the reality. Sometimes you have to make very tough choices.

The result from a given decision may be just what you hoped for and then again, you may experience the direct opposite. You cannot think about it enough, pray enough, or do enough research to guarantee that there is always a happy ending.

Listen to me when I tell you that there is no shortage of well-meaning people who will try to convince you otherwise. If you buy into their rhetoric or pressure, you will find yourself second-guessing every single choice that you make. Don't lose sight of the fact that the purveyors of such wisdom are rarely doing anything to assist you other than providing you with unsolicited advice and criticism.

So what's a caregiver to do?

Given your specific situation, you make the best choice you can with the information you have. And then you rest. You wait and see what happens. Observe and evaluate, knowing that if you must, you can make a different choice.

Do not waste your time judging the choice, as choices are not good or bad. They are simply decisions with results. If the results do not meet your expectations, try something else and see what happens. You have to face your individual circumstances. Face them, embrace them, and make the choice regardless of difficulty. I often contemplated a role reversal and what I would wish someone would choose for me. Sometimes that helped and other times I simply had to choose. Hard choices are just that—hard.

You can always make another choice when it is necessary.

CHAPTER 43

FROM REALITY TO RELEASE

No matter how sick or tired, I was allowed no time to rest. My voice had evaporated, replaced by a painfully sore throat and deep, wracking cough. If I could sleep, I thought I would get well, but lying down fueled my hi-speed thinking, stopping any possibility of rest. Feeling ill and without a voice or the ability to sleep, I had to keep going.

The day after moving my mother to the nursing home, I applied for government assistance because all funds were finally exhausted. I had stretched the money as far as I could. Feeling utterly humiliated, I stood in line waiting to be assigned a caseworker who viewed me, not as a grieving daughter, but as just another assigned number on a file folder.

Going through the motions of filling out papers again and answering questions amplified the already acute feeling of failure, as though I were on trial for being a bad daughter. Then came the waiting to see if Mom qualified for assistance. If not, I had no idea what would happen.

The nursing home personnel suggested I limit my visits at the nursing home for a few days, hoping that Mom's orientation to new people and routine would be smoother without me. Those days were filled with phone calls from the nursing home staff, social workers and occasionally a family member. Each call required energy that I simply didn't have. The nurses requested different clothing for Mom. Each social worker was trying to find a way to help my mother adjust to new surroundings and wanted my input. Family members wanted me to make them feel comfortable with the winter of my mother's life. The stress of dealing with everything depleted my body further and further.

After several days, when I finally felt a little stronger, I saw my mother for the first time since the move. She was frightened and begged me to let her **go home**. At first I thought Mom was talking about going home with me until I remembered that during the last few weeks in her apartment, she often wanted to **go home**. As we spent time together, no matter how much I tried to distract her, the conversation always circled back to her desperation to **go home**. I finally realized that she meant she did not wish to live any longer. She wanted to **go HOME**. Mom pleaded for my help to leave this life—something I could not give her.

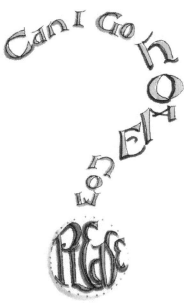

Mom had lost her anchor to reality, so during our visits I met my mother wherever she was. Her physical body was present, yet her mind freely wandered. Some days we were in a nightclub, according to Mom, and other days she was in a hospital. Anxiety washed over her as she spoke of the horrible people who were mean to her. In the midst of her profound confusion, she still recognized the lattés (her favorite "Ooh La La!") I brought with me. Mom seemed to recall the treat that we had so often enjoyed in the past. Her confusion seemed to come from her inability to separate past and current events. One of Mom's many concerns was not remembering when her mother died, so I searched for words to comfort without correcting. As we sipped our lattés, we talked. I held her hand and wrapped her in reassurance. Mostly, I just loved her and sometimes, even that wasn't enough.

In our first meeting, the nursing home physician and I discussed Mom's overpowering anxiety. Throughout the years of caring for her, I had never seen her so swallowed up and debilitated by her emotions. Sadness welled up as I spoke to the doctor of the journey my mother and I had taken together. He listened intently, making notes, and then turned his attention to Mom.

As if someone reached inside and flipped a switch inside of my mother, a pleasant personality emerged. Mystified by the sudden shift, I just observed Mom and tried to close my gaping mouth. Sitting in her wheelchair, my 94-year-old mother then actually ogled the young, handsome doctor! Mom had never flirted with anyone in her life that I knew about, and I began to really wonder where my mother was as I surely didn't recognize **this** woman!

Mom had lived at the nursing home for only a couple of weeks when, much to my shock, THE EXQUISITE TORTURER arrived. I happened upon the two of them during one of my visits. Mom looked at me with eyes that screamed fear as she began saying strange things to me. Mom exclaimed, "You must shake hands with her. You girls have to be friends." Her words tore through my heart. Mom knew better than anyone how THE EXQUISITE TORTURER had punished both of us for years with her hateful spoken words, letters, and gossip. As THE EXQUISITE TORTURER watched, I reacted only from instinct, putting my hand over Mom's heart.

Quietly, I said, "Mom, you know how much I love you. You know the truth. If you just put your hand here on your heart, you'll feel my love for you right there." I repeated the words until my reassurance and physical touch calmed and dissolved her immediate apprehension.

Refusing to witness any additional attempt by THE TORTURER to manipulate my mother's emotions, I kissed Mom and left. My reserves to fight and protect were sorely lacking.

A few days after seeing THE EXQUISITE TORTURER with my mother, I received yet another phone call. This time the Hospice social worker called to ask why I was spending so much time with my mother. I assured her that I was not doing that at all. "In fact," I explained, "I'm trying to stay home to get well so I don't infect my mother with whatever my body is fighting." The social worker reported that someone was staying with my mother from very early morning until late into the evening. Such lengthy visits were interfering with my mother's care and adjustment to her new surroundings. In my state of shock, I could not imagine who could be doing such a thing.

The day after my conversation with the social worker I learned the identity of my mother's visitor. It was my sister, THE EXQUISITE TORTURER, the one responsible for so much of our angst during the previous five years. Through our tears and talking, Mom and I recovered from each attack, while THE TORTURER just waited for signs of vulnerability. Her pattern of contact was unpredictable, but the emotional bombs she launched always found their targets—our hearts. Erroneously, I felt that THE EXQUISITE TORTURER would tire of the game of pretending to be a loving daughter and disappear just as she had in the past. The attention she gained from being so devoted in public was sure to wane, sending her back to her own life and out of ours.

But, this time THE TORTURER'S game was different. My mother had spiraled into some other dimension where truth was obscured and she was no longer able to express her opinion. Two doctors examined and declared her incompetent to make

decisions on her own. Responsibility weighed more heavily than ever, as now I had to rely solely on my own judgment. Mom could no longer help.

As the events of the next two weeks unfolded, a twilight zone enveloped me. THE EXQUISITE TORTURER garnered forces from the semi-cohesive family unit. She carefully wove a fabric of lies and deception with just enough truth for them to swallow her story causing them to evolve into a wild-eyed, vengeful family tribe. And each day, she spent my mother's every waking moment with her.

Phone calls to my home intensified. There were so many long, haranguing messages from various members of the tribe that I disconnected my answering machine and no longer picked up the receiver. I could not reason with their demands to bring my mother back to her apartment. They would not listen to any explanation about the level of care Mom now required. SANCTIMONIOUS SHIRLEY even begged me to release my mother into the care of THE EXQUISITE TORTURER! At that moment, even in my compromised state, I laughed at the thought.

Then the assaults accelerated. With spewing accusations, THE TORTURER captured anyone with ears: nurses, former caregivers, Hospice workers and nursing home staff. A few of them, loyal to my mother, repeated my sister's venomous words to me. Beginning to grasp what THE EXQUISITE TORTURER was doing, my twilight zone exploded.

As one maneuver failed, THE EXQUISITE TORTURER tried another. She and her husband took my obviously rehearsed mother to the office of the nursing home administrator. Haltingly, my mother repeated, "I want to take away those papers from my girl and give them to this girl and then I want to go with them." According to the report from the administrator, after saying those words, my mom looked at my sister and asked, "Is that right?"

I was shocked by their tactic, but after speaking with an elder-care attorney, I felt that Mom was safe where she was and decided the best response was to ignore THE EXQUISITE TORTURER and her husband. They had no power.

Curiously, one day after the attempted and failed coercion of my mother, both the nursing home and I were anonymously reported for state investigations, insinuating abuse of my mother. After a brief investigation, all allegations were dropped, and I thought the nonsense was over.

To be sure that I was doing everything necessary to care for Mom, I contacted her attorney for advice. He had created all the legal paperwork for both of my parents and I hope that he might be able to do something to protect Mom from any further manipulation. We spent several hours discussing his opinion and what needed to be done. At his suggestion, enacting my power of attorney, I banned the tribe from the nursing home for a long weekend so Mom could rest, and hopefully find some peace of mind. I called to check on her several times and learned that she had calmed down and seemed quite happy. Mom's anxiety level had diminished and she was comfortably resting. I hoped in vain that the assaults had stopped.

After my mother's undisturbed weekend, the Hospice social worker came to my home to discuss a plan for incorporating the family tribe into Mom's life.

Reflecting about our previous five years together, I thought about how most of the family members chose to participate in Mom's life from a distance, only, and missed watching her blossom into her amazing self with a terrific sense of humor, strong opinions, and independence for the first time in her life.

By the time the tribe saw their own need to connect with Mom, she was already well along the path to her inner world. The tribe had had unlimited access to Mom, yet rarely took advantage of their opportunities. When Mom lived with us, several of them explained that I made them far too uncomfortable for them to visit in her apartment. Mom's response to them was, "I have my own door. It's **my** apartment and you can see me anytime that you want to."

Mom often talked to me about her feelings of rejection by her family. When I couldn't listen any longer, I employed a psychologist who came to our home to help her sort it all out.

During all the months that Mom lived in assisted living, THE EXQUISITE TORTURER had never even taken her out for a cup of coffee. When visiting nearby tribal members during the holidays, THE EXQUISITE TORTURER refused to see Mom and rarely phoned her. MANIPULATED MICHELE, who lived within 30 minutes of her grandmother, managed to keep her first visit in thirteen months to a matter of moments. My mother always felt that obligation was the reason for such visits as she was never the destination but rather a short stop en route to the real destination—shopping or visiting some other tribal member. But now we had to schedule time for each individual person to visit Mom!

Somehow by creating a sense of urgency, the leader of the pack had whipped them into a frenzy, sending an even deeper shock wave through my soul.

Mom's attorney had also strongly suggested that we have a family meeting with an objective outsider. I agreed, as I saw no other logical alternative. I asked the Hospice social worker to facilitate the mediation, but just as we were deciding on the date, the social worker received a call from her office. She told me that The EXQUISITE TORTURER had called the nursing home as well as the Hospice office, demanding a family meeting on her terms. Too tired at that moment to flex my legal muscle, I abided by THE EXQUISITE TORTURER's day and time.

The day of mediation arrived. Still struggling with a sick body I dressed myself in white clothes from head to toe, hoping that somehow I could deflect the poisonous tribal energy that was sure to be present. Climbing into my car I prepared to take the same short drive I had taken with my mother only a few weeks earlier. This time I felt like I was driving five hundred miles to a death sentence.

I pulled into the nursing home lot and parked my car.

As I left my vehicle, I took only my keys and a small package of tissues. With a friend for support rather than my husband, whom I knew would feel an overwhelming need to protect and defend me, I entered the intensely charged room and sat down.

Quickly scanning the room, I was relieved that my mother was not in attendance to hear what was sure to be a difficult conversation revolving around her.

I reluctantly looked into the eyes of the tribe: WEAK WANDA, THE EXQUISITE TORTURER and granddaughter, MANIPULATED MICHELE. Apparently, MANIPULATED MICHELE was the stand-in for SANCTIMONIOUS SHIRLEY who, once again, didn't make an appearance. Sitting beside each of my sisters and my niece were their husbands. Each pair of eyes, in one brief moment, told me their story of disdain and suspicion.

Being in a room behind a closed door with all of them felt as though the air had been replaced by putrid, lethal gas. The quiet, stoic spirit within me was choking and struggled to continue breathing.

Trying to open the dialogue between the tribal members and their spouses, the social worker began.

"We're here today to discuss how each of you can best deal with your mother and grandmother," she said, with a compassionate voice. She continued, "To begin with, I'd like to hear from each of you. How do you see yourself augmenting her life here at the nursing home?"

The tribal members looked at each other in confusion. They had no intention of augmenting my mother's life and began searching for words to explain what a ridiculous idea that was.

Real dialogue never happened. Representatives from the nursing home as well as several of the Hospice team struggled to maintain professional demeanor as accusations of inadequate care were hurled at them by the tribe.

Then one of the more vocal tribesman, THE EXQUISITE TORTURER'S HUSBAND, interrupted the stilted conversation to explain the real reason for their attendance.

"Our one and only purpose today is to remove my mother-in-law from the 'hell-hole' into which **she** placed her," he said, thrusting a finger at me. With great emphasis he continued, "And, we have brought our vehicles and are going to accomplish this goal today!" In total disbelief at what I was hearing, my mind flashed on the recollection that only a few months before, he had moved his own mother against her will to live in the same town with him and my sister—straight into a nursing home!

I could not seem to comprehend what I was hearing. Their distorted words sounded stretched out like a scene playing in slow motion.

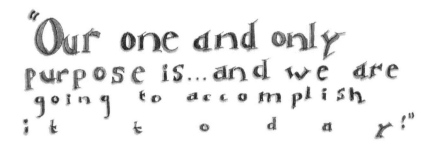

The social worker spoke quietly and said, "That is not the reason that we are here in this meeting. We are here to discuss how each of you can help this dear lady enjoy her life here."

MANIPULATED MICHELE'S HUSBAND, glowing bright red, nearly levitated above his chair as he glared at me and through his clenched teeth hissed, "You should be ashamed of yourself! Your mother bought and paid for that apartment on **your** house and the least you can do is to let her live in it!"

I was stunned as I watched my sisters and niece mutely agree with their spouses as each of them hurled insults toward me and everyone who was involved with my mother's care.

Once again, the social worker tried to regain control, looked at the men and said to THE EXQUISITE TORTURER'S HUSBAND, "I understand that everyone has an opinion about why your mother-in-law is now living here. But, the fact remains that due to the level of care she requires, her daughter," nodding my direction, "feels that this is the best place for her."

Not to be outdone, WEAK WANDA'S HUSBAND glowered at me as he spoke in broken English, "I'm part of this family already five year and never seen no more disrespect! I want to know exactly why not she can move from here right this moment!"

The social worker remained silent for a moment as if to decipher what she had heard from WEAK WANDA'S HUSBAND. Then she nodded toward me again and said, "You cannot move her because she is the only one with the authority to make such decisions. She is the one with the legal paperwork."

WEAK WANDA'S HUSBAND nearly jumped out of his seat as he boomed, "What paperwork? I never seen no paperwork!"

"Sir, I have not only seen the paperwork, I have copies of it and so does her file here at the nursing home," the social worker said, trying once again to diffuse the volatile situation.

When given the information that moving my mother was impossible without my consent, my family's collective emotions erupted.

The tribe then starred in their own circus, complete with clowns and mirrors that distorted the truth. Questions based in ignorance flew around the room. "Do you realize what a horrible bed she has? Her mattress is filled with nothing but lumps." "She's only one little old woman and she's not on IV fluids or catheterized, so how hard can it be to care for her?" And, ill-informed statements like, "We have all the wherewithal and all the resources to make her comfortable in her last days." And with fingers pointed my direction, "There is no one in this family causing any problems but **HER!**"

I was so glad that my husband did not see the tribal spectacle or hear their words. There was enough pain tearing through my heart without having to see it reflected in his eyes, as well.

I removed myself emotionally from the meeting and retreated inside to survive. In those surreal moments, I could not absorb how much my own family distrusted me. These were my sisters with whom I had shared holidays and the births of our children, as well as the pain of their multiple broken relationships. Taking in the intensity of their collective hatred for me was unfathomable.

Absolutely nothing was accomplished during the family beating other than completely anesthetizing my heart.

Realizing that they could not remove my mother that day, THE EXQUISITE TORTURER called off the meeting. She donned a smile and showed her other face by giving the false impression that they would all agree to suggestions from the social worker by stating, "Why of course, we will agree to scheduled visits as long as **she** is not present. After all, we just want what is best for Mom." With that, as if on cue, the tribe stood up to leave.

As WEAK WANDA passed by, she reached to touch me as she squeaked, "You know, I still love you," when only moments before she had been nodding her head in agreement with her husband and the others. The incongruence of her words and actions seared through my soul assassinating any hope for a future relationship.

Unsure whether my legs would carry me, I remained in my chair until their exodus was complete. My friend encircled me with her arms and helped me to my feet. Together we walked down the long hallway, out the door, and through the whispering tribal circle that had gathered just outside the nursing home. As I walked through the circle, a sudden hush closed their mouths and no one said a word to me. In that moment, I hoped that I might be experiencing a nightmare. In vain I tried to will myself awake only to finally accept that the nightmare was reality. Looking straight ahead, I opened a car door, hoping I was getting into my car as anything familiar had vanished.

In silence, my friend and I drove away. Having lived through one of the worst events of my life, I just wanted to be somewhere else—anywhere else. I couldn't get to my husband fast enough. I needed to know that someone—anyone—still loved me.

The day after the meeting I received a phone call. THE EXQUISITE TORTURER managed to convince her minions that they should hire an attorney to begin legal proceedings against me in order to get control of Mom. The voice on the phone was their new attorney calling with ridiculous demands based on the lies of the tribe. He told me that they intended to secure a court order to remove my mother from the nursing home so as to place her with them.

They planned to have her declared competent by a doctor of their choosing in order to rescind any authority that I thought I had. And then *Mr. Attorney* asked me how I planned to respond. Respond? How could I respond? I had no words left.

When one attorney failed, they hired others. **Each one represented the family of my mother**. Hearing those words and reading them on paper, made me realize that I was excluded not only from my family, but also from my mother.

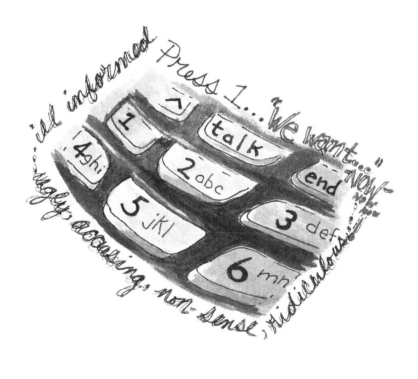

I felt like a caged animal being poked by the sharp sticks of their words and actions, leaving deep, gaping wounds behind. Their tactics and assaults continued for weeks. The only instinct I had left was sheer survival. I had to make an unbearable choice.

The pain of my choice defies expression.

My entire life encompassed shared genetics and history with the people I called **family**. They had left no doubt that now I was no longer part of them. Comprehending the obvious hatred that my **family** felt for me was immeasurable. These were the people that assured me they would always support me, no matter what. THE EXQUISITE TORTURER, herself, faithfully reminded me throughout my entire life that I couldn't count on anyone but my **family**. Trying to defend myself in the face of insufferable assaults, their destructive attacks, and the prospect of a legal battle that would only serve to tear my mother into pieces and shred my withering spirit... I had only one choice... I could think of only one thing to do.

My mother's attorney drafted an agreement that required the entire tribe and their spouses to sign. Nine people in three different states had to agree to have no written, verbal or physical contact with me or my husband. The agreement was forever. If they took control of my mother, they must all agree never to contact us again. In turn, I would walk away.

Incessant questions were stuck in my mind, repeating over and over without stopping. "How did the tribe beat me into submission? How did this happen? How did I let them win? Why did I cave in? How could I ever exist inside my own skin? How could I go on living, knowing that my mother was with them? Would they take care of her? Would they touch her? Calm her? Meet her where she was?"

I had no answers... no words... nothing...

My decision tore through my heart like a multimillion-volt lightning strike leaving behind only the pain of being electrocuted and blown apart.

Somewhere in the silence of my brokenness, panic swept over me when I realized that I couldn't remember the last time I saw my mother's face... listened to her voice... witnessed the way she brightened when I walked into her presence. I had no memory of what I last said to her or what she said to me. I couldn't remember if she was calm or frightened. I couldn't find the memory. My husband tried to help me remember. My friend tried to help me. But it simply was not there. No memory. Nothing at all. Nothing remained but a hole in my heart shaped like Mom and me.

My husband watched, helplessly, not knowing what to do but cradle me in his arms. Without him, I was certain that I would cease to be. Breathing required conscious effort. I was sure that if I took my awareness away, my lungs would stop trying to take in air because it hurt to breathe. My hands hurt. My head hurt. Everything hurt. Food wouldn't move down my throat. My heart pounded as if trying to rip its way out of my chest. Every muscle in my body tightened until I thought my bones were pulling apart. My eyes ached. I couldn't stand to see anything that reminded me of my mother or anyone in my family.

As quickly as I could, I packed away all pictures, gifts Mom had given me, anything with her handwriting and most of my memories. Somehow, I knew that if I didn't get everything out of my sight, I would burn it all.

And then fear took over. I was afraid to be alone and terrified to go anywhere. What if someone innocently asked, "How are you?" or worse, "How is your mother doing?" I had no answers. No words. Only pain... shredded remains of my soul... gaping wounds ... pain... and failure.

Everyone signed the document. Not even **one** person hesitated or questioned why such an action was needed. Within 24 hours, the document was signed and returned to my mother's attorney.

The ringing of my phone pierced the silence and, from that far too-familiar distant place, I listened as the attorney delivered the report.

THE EXQUISITE TORTURER took possession of Mom and removed her from the nursing home and from me. THE EXQUISITE TORTURER then deposited my mother in MANIPULATED MICHELE's home with her husband and their two young children.

and...

...With nothing left, I let go of my mom.

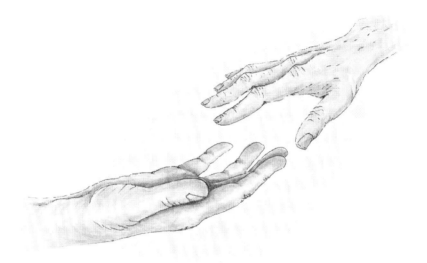

REFLECTION

SELF-PRESERVATION

There are no guarantees in this life. You many have been conditioned by your family, authority figures, or even your church that if you are good enough and make the right choices, everything will go smoothly for you. This kind of thinking creates fantasies with happily-ever-after endings. Unfortunately, there are no guarantees, only outcomes.

At this point in my story, I'm sure you are finding yourself feeling very glad that you are you, and not me! I don't blame you one bit for thinking that. In fact, I would rather be you and not me, too. Believe it or not, there is another tool to gather for your caregiving tool belt hidden beneath all the emotion of my ultimate decision.

That tool is called self-preservation. I wish I could tell you that I had been visited by God who gave me permission to save myself, but that would be a fable.

During one of the last discussions with my mother's attorney, he made a simple observation. "This is killing you." He was right. It was killing me, and I had to admit it. His next statement proved equally powerful. "I know how much you love your mother, but you don't owe her your life."

In that moment, I could no longer feel anything, but I could still think. Many of my thoughts teetered on irrationality, but insisted on being heard anyway. Maybe I should simply let the weight of the whole situation kill me and be done with it. After all, how could an entire group of people called **family** hate me so much unless I was positively evil? The questions and thoughts marched on and on.

Even in that crazy state of mind, I took the time I needed to give myself permission to live or die. I could leave this life for whatever comes next or choose to save myself and see what happened.

By reading my story, you know the choice I made. I saved myself. Over time I became a little more comfortable with my choice. Even now, if I allow myself to wander back to the point where I made my conscious decision for self-preservation, I cannot stay for long. While there, I choose **again** to let go of wanting things that I will never have: my family's approval and oneness with them. As those wants float away on my imaginary kite, I come back to today where I live and love. I revisit the treasured memories of my mother and me. I spend time with my son and my husband. I watch my grandchildren explore life. I shore up relationships with my friends—my true family.

No matter what anyone tells you, it is okay to save yourself.
Give yourself permission.
You are worth it.

CHAPTER 44

FROM HELL TO HEALING

The tribe took what was left of my mother when I gave up her remaining physical possessions. I could have fought for them, but the tribe seemed to think that the collection of Mom's things would make her feel familiar in totally strange surroundings. I had no fight left, and I knew that their motive for claiming her things was more about hurting me than comforting Mom. It was only stuff… trinkets… bits… and stuff. I could let go of it all because everything of real value remained somewhere within me.

Strangers, friends of the tribe, arrived with trucks and trailers and came to my door to remove my mother's belongings and, if possible, my memories. The strangers rang the doorbell intending to show me a printed list of everything the tribe demanded. They had been given specific instructions to go through my home in order to fill their vehicles with everything from the list. Much to their

dismay, we had placed all of my mother's things in piles on the driveway, in anticipation of their arrival.

From the window we watched them make frantic cell phone calls because their plan had gone awry. Then we watched them carry my mother's jewelry box and drop it in the grass. We watched as they demolished her glass curio cabinet by knocking it over on the concrete driveway. After several agonizing hours, the group of buffoons, loaded with their booty, finally drove away.

Somewhere in all of the insanity of those first weeks without my mother, a vivid dream came to me. She and I were walking together on a lovely road. Mom was considerably younger — much as I remembered her when I was a young mother. We walked together arm in arm, laughing and talking and reminiscing.

Suddenly, a fork in the road appeared, and I didn't know which way we should go. My mother stopped and looked past my eyes, into my soul and said, "It's time for me to go now. You will be just fine." She hugged and kissed me and simply said, "I love you."

I have no recollection of being sad. I simply accepted her decision.

The dream helped me through many tough moments when I struggled to find a reason to hang on to my life. Seeing mom with such clarity gave me something to fill the vacant space where I had no memory of seeing her for the last time. It was a beautiful dream, with Mom's permission and encouragement to go on with my life.

And so my journey toward healing began.

The intensity of the anxiety attacks I experienced eventually lessened and disappeared, leaving behind nothing but emptiness and a body that no longer felt anything. After a few weeks of stumbling around trying to find something to orient me back into my life, I sought out my former psychologist. I wanted her to make me accountable—to assign a routine—to help me get back to anything that felt like normal. I asked her to give me a list of things to order my day. I wanted her to somehow anchor me into life. Instead, she told me that I needed to, "sit in the stew of my emotions." I recoiled at what I considered awful advice. As time went by, I grew to accept that by refusing to feel my emotions, they waited. And lurked. I could feel them when they showed up or wait til later. It was my choice.

Sitting in the silent stew, feeling what I felt, occupied most of my time for months.

The revolving door of people had stopped, and the incessantly ringing phone quieted. I was alone with my wandering thoughts and feelings for the first time in years.

My emotions multiplied when people who didn't know what had happened asked about my mom. It happened over and over and over... at the grocery store... at the gym... at the mall. The inquiry always evoked complete disbelief, followed by sadness to each of us, leaving an even deeper chasm in my heart. Each of my acquaintances knew the relationship between Mom and me and, as we spoke, I could not begin to camouflage my feelings.

To avoid the questions, I avoided people. I was nearly housebound, yet I couldn't stand to be home. Sometimes I didn't know where I was. Sometimes I would sleep all day and stay up most of the night. I had no routine. I was in limbo, haunted by the thoughts of my mother and where she was. I needed my mother to be free so that the tribe could no longer manipulate, convincing her that I didn't love or care about her.

I spent hours writing letters to Mom that I never mailed. I needed to tell her how much I missed her and loved her. Our past conversations, experiences and memories replayed in an endless loop in my mind.

The journey back to myself was hell. Surrender was the first step out of the hell toward a new life. I could not change what had happened, but I didn't have to let it destroy me. I can't remember how or when, but I surrendered to the moment, allowing me to begin the move out of the horrifying, tortured place where I was trapped. I somehow accepted that the only way out of the pain was to walk through it.

Out of desperation, I searched for and found a grief support group. Every person attending had lost someone, but no one had encountered a loss like mine. It felt so ugly, strange and incomplete. My story had no ending. Without judging, everyone accepted me, ugliness and all. The group was united by profound loss and determination to somehow, once again, find meaning in life. Just being with others who spoke with compassion allowed me to move forward in the healing process.

A few months after the tribe took Mom and her possessions, we turned the apartment, built solely for the purpose of creating a home for her, into an art studio. Sometimes I could go there and try my hand at creating something; sometimes I went there, only to turn around and leave the space. The pain was still omnipresent, and it hid in every corner.

Little by little, I recovered my health and I found strength again. Feeling my way along, I kept moving. I sought out people to work on my body to ease it along the road to physical wellness. Massages and chiropractic treatments helped. A homeopathic practitioner assisted my emotional healing through the gentle art of flower essences and homeopathy.

Every day, I waited. I waited for a phone call that my mother was free. I subscribed to the newspaper so that I could read her obituary because I was certain that no one from the tribe would contact me when she was gone. Somehow I was able to hang on through the moments when I felt total failure and despair envelop me. I waited and I waited.

Weeks turned into months as spring and summer arrived. In all previous years I had turned our yard into a beautiful park because my mother loved it so. She could see the bright colors and watch the birds from her window or from her chair on the deck beneath her beloved oak tree. This year, all laid fallow. My mother was not here to see our yard, yet I knew that she was still somewhere.

I continued to wait. The few weeks that the tribe thought Mom would live, stretched into nearly 12 months. Twelve hollow, unresolved, grief-stricken months. Twelve months of waiting. I never before realized how difficult waiting could be.

Rather than caring for Mom, THE EXQUISITE TORTURER spent her time constructing elaborate

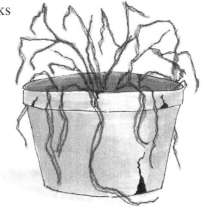

notebooks of embellished evidence against me that she intended to use to prove her imaginary case of theft and ill-gotten gain I'd received by preying on our parents.

I spent the months waiting and missing my mother. I missed her ninety-fifth birthday and Thanksgiving and Christmas and Valentine's Day and Easter and Mother's Day.

The truth was that I had missed Mom much longer than twelve months. Each time she walked away from me into her secret inner world, I missed her. Her body was with me, yet so often her mind was elsewhere. One day through the endless river of tears, I realized what I **really** missed about my mother.

I missed the way her eyes always lit up when I walked into the room. No matter how difficult the day or how many decisions I had wrestled, her eyes brightened when she saw me and I knew that I was doing exactly what I wanted to do—caring for my mother and building my true inheritance of memories, conversations, and experiences. Each experience we shared belongs to me. Each conversation that surfaced helped me heal. Each memory gave me the courage to hang on when it would have been so easy to let go. Each and every memory remained with me, untouchable by anyone.

And so I continued to wait…

Acknowledging how much my life had been swallowed up by caregiving required courage. I wrestled with the reality that everything which defined me and made my heart sing, no longer existed. My music remained silent. My piano, long out of tune, collected dust. My fabric and projects laid in disorganized piles around my sewing machine, and the paints hardened in their tubes. My business now existed only in my imagination, leaving behind potential unexplored avenues, and a sore lack of income. But the greatest void was my teaching. I had been teaching something to someone since I was sixteen years old. I needed to teach. It was the best part of me; teaching fueled my soul.

The years of caring for my parents changed everything, as caregiving required me to let go of it all. I didn't lose everything at once. It was a slow process, like a slow leak… being depleted while nothing restocked my creative spirit. Once there was a wealth of ideas and activity bubbling inside me. In its place remained a vacuum.

My life had been totally remodeled in order to become a caregiver. And then I realized that my last defining role, **caregiver**, I also lost.

Somehow, after the complete loss of everything—my parents, my family, my creativity, my career—I slowly opened my heart to a new realization. I could be anything because I was a clean slate. It was time to begin the process of finally finding **me** again. Although my thoughts never strayed far away from my mother, hour by hour… day by day, I tentatively explored who I could become. I learned to be patient with myself allowing each small step to bring me fulfillment.

One day in late summer I was offered an opportunity to create my ideal job. The day I accepted the offer was the day I agreed to begin teaching again. All the months of counseling and grief support came to an end, because it was time to go on with my life. My creative spirit began to resurface as I slowly designed my life anew.

The first day that I actually stepped in front of a class, I stopped waiting.

And that was the very day my mother was set free.

Mom's attorney called to tell me. Although she had passed in the morning hours, I was not notified until the late afternoon when I was sitting with my husband sipping coffee. We were sitting on the same bench where we sat every day for our afternoon date. Mom understood that our coffee date kept us connected to each other and insisted that my husband and I keep our commitment to our mini-respite from the day's events. Mom not only understood our coffee date, sometimes she joined us on that bench. She loved being with us, sharing an "Ooh La La!" and then later exhausted me as she recounted "our date," moment by moment.

I had been asked many times how I would feel when I knew that Mom was free. Of course, no one can know the answer to a question like that. But, even I was surprised at my reaction to the knowledge of her passing. Sitting on that bench, hearing the news, I was elated! I knew that she was truly free, and so was I. How amazing that I learned of her freedom in such a significant place.

Mom and I could once again meet in my dreams to talk about everything just as we so often did during our mornings on the deck. I was free to pursue my life. She was free, at last, to go on to whatever happens next.

The rawest months of healing were behind me. There was life after death. I knew, not because someone told me or because the Bible said so, but because I lived it.

Eleven months after my mother's death, thick evidential three-ring binders were presented by my sister to a detective in the police department in hopes of pressing a criminal case against me for abusing my mother. As requested, I arrived at the appointment and after being ushered into an interrogation room, I was read my Miranda rights, and once again entered a twilight zone.

The somewhat nervous detective began his questioning. "Your family wants to know exactly where your mother's wedding rings are." Reaching into the small bag beside my chair, I retrieved my mother's journal and opened to the page where she wrote,

"… as for my wedding rings, I wish my grandson who lives in California to have them. I told him this and I have given them to him and I'm writing it here, as well, because this is my desire." Beside the entry was a date and Mom's initials.

The detective turned his attention to a check register that THE EXQUISITE TORTURER had pieced together where she had highlighted all my "suspicious expenditures." He said, "I see here that checks were written to a trainer at a gym. Can you explain that?" Leafing through Mom's journal, my hand stopped and I looked at the page.

I read, "I have instructed my daughter to use my money to pay for the exercises that she takes at the gym. This helps her to stay strong so she can take care of me. This is my wish." Beside the entry, again, was a date and her signature.

Several times while Mom lived with me, she expressed her profound concern about THE EXQUISITE TORTURER's behavior. Mom was afraid that she might try to "give me trouble." In addition to frequently recording her thoughts and desires in journals, Mom directed her attorney to amend all legal documents as an attempt to leave no doubt about her wishes and to stem any future problems her daughter was likely to cause.

In spite of it all, there I was sitting in a small room with a ring attached to the wall where criminals were handcuffed, suffering the humiliation of interrogation and knowing that I could actually go on trial for caring for my parents.

Following Mom and Dad's direction, creating the existence that they desired, suddenly seemed foolish.

The questioning continued for more than four exhausting hours as the detective probed the details of my nearly debilitating caregiving journey. My mind eventually went blank and as if I'd stepped away from my body, I began to realize that each time the detective asked about something, my mother answered. Through her legal documents and hand written journals, one by one, Mom addressed the detective's concerns from beyond her grave.

One day later, the investigation was dropped.

WEAK WANDA and SANCTIMONIOUS SHIRLEY continued living their lives as if nothing unusual had occurred in our family, praying that their vindictive sister didn't single out either of them in the future. Within a few weeks of her grandmother's death, MANIPULATED MICHELE moved her family as far from THE EXQUISITE TORTURER as possible, leaving her aunt unsupported in the choice of her next target.

As for me... I am finally alive again.

Now, I spend hours in our studio, creating with passion. I find comfort and peace where I previously only found pain. As I work on my art, my mind replays memories of the journey caring for my parents. The years of caregiving were filled with challenges and choices beyond anything I could have anticipated. Now I can't help but smile when I think my mom plays little tricks on us in our studio. She loved that space more than any place on this earth, and now, so do I.

Just like the mythological Phoenix, who is said to regenerate from the fire when hurt or wounded by a foe, I too rose from the ashes—changed, but better.

I thought I had forgotten what it felt like to live and laugh. I discovered that I didn't forget. I was reborn, seeing everything with new eyes. While I was a focused caregiver, the world changed and I hadn't found time to notice. Entire subdivisions and shopping centers had sprung up. Even the brightness of lights on buildings amazed me. Technology had grown by leaps and bounds and everything around me beckoned for attention. My eyes and spirit embraced everything... each sight... each experience... as though I'd never existed before.

Once again I have a life. It's definitely not the life that I used to have. It is a new life where I love more completely and value relationships more deeply. With determination and help, I slowly found my way again.

During one of my last counseling sessions, my psychologist asked, "If you had the benefit of hindsight, what would you have chosen to do differently?"

I remained silent, searching my heart…

… and then clarity…

"I would change nothing."

I realized that each and every experience I shared with my parents, no matter how difficult, was stitched into the fabric of my life with threads of gratitude. Every choice I made, every experience I shared, every truth I learned refined me, leading me into peace and gratitude.

My life is the sum of my choices and I am grateful!

REFLECTION

IT TAKES AS LONG AS IT TAKES

I remember someone in my grief support group asking how long the grief process usually lasted. Responses from the group included, "At least a year" or, "I don't know." I read books and searched the Internet for better answers. My psychologist once told me that my grief process was complex and I could not bear to believe that working through healing might be so open-ended. I needed to know somehow that I wouldn't always feel so pain-filled.

In my searching, I found the answer. It wasn't the answer I expected, but as time goes by, it has proven to be accurate. The answer to the question is, **"It takes as long as it takes."** Neither you nor I can hurry it or slow it down. The process has a pace dependent on individuality and circumstances.

Grief is a response to an experience of loss. It's a process — an inevitable part of life. Common symptoms of grief may include feeling numb, lacking concentration, disrupted sleeping and eating, gaining weight, relapses into old habits and roller coaster emotions. **These are not stages of grief. They are symptoms or responses to grief.**

Grief is as individual as the person feeling the grief. Never let anyone give you the one-size-fits-all explanation for how you are feeling. Everyone has his or her own experience. The intensity varies from one person to another as there are no absolutes in the grieving process. Please be gentle and take care of yourself.

You do have some control in what seems to be an uncontrollable situation. As you walk along this life path, do your best to keep reality in your sights. The person you are grieving was human, not divine. Try not to remodel that person into someone other than who he or she was. Do your best to maintain a foothold in the here and now. By that, I mean stay present and celebrate the life of your loved one and the role he or she played in your life.

When you feel sad, it's natural to cry. But, if you cry without stopping, you probably need to get some help. If you use artificial means to dull the pain for an extended period of time, that's a cue for outside help, too. You know yourself better than anyone else, so stay in tune. When you can, take control over that which is controllable.

Decide not to become stuck in your grief, a state that given enough time may even paralyze you. Getting stuck in the trauma or shock associated with loss is more common than you might think. Recognize that the grief process is a layered process with no set way to "get over it." Just be where you are and when you are ready, begin moving forward, taking steps toward healing as you can.

Time itself does not heal but time is necessary to recover from the shock and trauma brought about by losing someone. You may find that specific dates trigger powerful memories. Try to recognize that dates don't have power. The memory has the power. Just let the memories show up as they will, and work on your healing from within. Do what's right for you.

Thank you for joining me on this journey. I wish you peace wherever you are. I leave you with the words of my friend.

"Always remember, it didn't come to stay, it came to pass."

∽ ∽ ♡ ∽ ∽

PART III

HINDSIGHT

HEALTH

HOPE

ME TIME

CARING FOR THE CAREGIVER

Caring for yourself should never be last on your list of things to do. Sadly, that's exactly what happens to most caregivers. If you don't maintain your mental, emotional and physical health, your caregiving experience will defeat you.

In caregiving lingo, you must have "me time" to continue providing adequate care for someone else. That means, every day you must carve out time to care for your physical body as well as your mental and emotional well-being. I know you may be saying to yourself, "There's no way that I can do one more thing!" Believe me, if you don't, you'll be in serious trouble as time goes on. This is not a luxury, its absolutely non-negotiable.

Stress took a toll during my years of being a caregiver. Caring for myself was a constant challenge. When I realized I was existing on the ragged edge, my determination to survive somehow kicked in. The following pages contain suggestions for "me time" based on my discoveries about self-care. Believe me when I tell you, I absolutely practiced what I'm preaching.

Please, please, please take the time to take care of yourself.

ME TIME (1)

FOOD AND NUTRITION

Quality Food and Supplements Really Count

Good Food:
Each of the suggestions regarding self care is important, but proper food and nutrition are the highest priority.

- ❀ The body can't function very long without adequate nutrition. It will keep going as long as it can, but eventually fatigue and illness take over.

- ❀ The body, if not well nourished, succumbs to depletion during times of added stress. Even with the very best nutrition on board, you may face challenges, but you will extend your longevity as a caregiver by caring for the mechanism you call your body.

Food is Fuel:
Food is fuel for the body, a fact that is often overlooked. Eating only what tastes good or foods that are easy to eat, often contain very little nutritive value. During stressful situations,

some people eat for comfort or to temporarily escape their stress. Highly processed foods and those high in sugar are often the first ones chosen. On the other hand, some people react to stress by hardly eating anything or only snacking without thought about the quality of the foods they are taking in. As a caregiver, you must give your fuel more conscious consideration.

Quality Protein:

The key to adequately fueling the body is to eat the best quality food you can find. If you have access to organic foods and grass-fed meats, you are well on your way to fueling your body in the best way possible. By consuming meat that is antibiotic and hormone free, your body is able to access the nutrition without using valuable resources to combat hidden chemicals. If you choose to obtain protein from non-animal sources, look at your options carefully and keep your diet as clean as you can.

Fruits and Vegetables:

If you have a farmer's market in your area, it's a great place to shop for seasonal fruits and vegetables. Look for produce that is organic and grown without pesticides. Just as with the meats, the cleaner the produce, the fewer undesirable substances your body has to deal with. Having said that, be sure to thoroughly wash all produce with some type of vegetable wash. Washing removes dirt and helps destroy parasites, invisible to the naked eye.

Grocery Store Shopping:

I encourage you to eat as many whole food as possible. Eating whole foods means eating the entire fresh apple or pear rather than their canned counterparts. One of the best things you can do is read labels. If you can't pronounce an ingredient or don't know what it is, don't eat it. When shopping in traditional grocery stores, the bulk of your shopping should be around the perimeter of the store. That's where you will find the least processed, boxed, canned and preserved foods.

Alternative Food Considerations:

As an active caregiver, I changed my diet to give my body every possible chance to stay healthy, and even today I eat the following foods very sparingly: wheat, white rice, corn, sugar, barley, rye, peanuts and pistachios. I still choose to keep these as "once in a while" foods because of our accepted storage methods (grains stored in huge silos for long periods of time or left in open containers exposed to weather, bugs, and more) and the susceptibility of some of these foods to mold. Better alternatives include, amaranth, quinoa, wild rice, stevia, coconut, almonds, walnuts, cashews, as well as raw sunflower seeds, pumpkin seeds, and pine nuts.

Supplements:

I highly recommend that you check out quality supplements. Daily multivitamins, immune boosters like Beta Glucan, probiotics (especially if you've taken lots of antibiotics), Omega 3 and garlic are some of my favorites.

Caregiver Pledge:

I pledge to nourish my body by eating the best foods because I am worth it.

Summary

- ❀ **Good Food** is essential, especially during times of additional stress caused by caregiving.

- ❀ **Food is Fuel** but beware, food is easily substituted as comfort or escape from stress.

- ❀ **Quality Protein** as grass-fed, hormone and antibiotic-free meat is best, but non-animal sources are also plentiful.

- ❀ **Fruits and Vegetables** raised without pesticides are best but should still be thoroughly washed.

- ❀ **Grocery Store Shopping** is best around the perimeter of the store to avoid highly processed foods.

- ❀ **Alternative Food Considerations** include amaranth, quinoa, wild rice, stevia, coconut, almonds, walnuts, cashews, as well as raw sunflower seeds, pumpkin seeds, and pine nuts.

- ❀ **Supplements** are recommended for optimal health.

- ❀ For additional information please visit, *http://www.HopeForCaregivers.com/**nutrition***

ME TIME (2)

EXERCISE

Movement and Massage Help You De-stress

Take Time:

I know, the last thing you have energy for or want to do is exercise, but I implore you to give it high priority. Stress is dramatically affected by exercise allowing you to feel better mentally as well as physically. What caregiver doesn't need that?

Stress Hormones:

Cortisol—an important hormone—is needed to keep the body functioning properly. It has also been called the stress hormone because the body secretes Cortisol during times of elevated stress. Problems begin to occur when the body remains in a state of stress over a long periods of time and seldom, if ever, returns to a state of relaxation. Prolonged elevated levels of hormones like Cortisol can wreak havoc on the body. To combat a perpetual state of stress, you must exercise.

Stress Relief and Strength:

Along with stress relief through exercise, building and maintaining strength is essential. Because many caregiving situations are progressive, the patient tends to become more dependent on his caregiver. By being physically strong, it may help keep you from sustaining injuries while supporting and helping your patient more around. If you don't maintain your strength, you can get hurt and then what will happen to the person you are caring for?

Exercise Suggestions:

It doesn't matter if you try something new or stick with a form of exercise that you like. Just do something! Consider walking, weight training, dancing, pilates or yoga to name a few. If you don't like to exercise, you may have to "learn to like it," as my mom said when I was growing up. It's that important.

Get Out of the House:

Although you can find ways to exercise without leaving home, I encourage you to get away from the caregiving environment whenever possible. A change of scenery and fresh air have remarkable mental as well as physical benefits, too.

Massage:

While you're caring for your body, schedule a massage, especially if you are exercising regularly. Massage is therapeutic, not just luxury. It helps your lymphatic system move toxins out of the body, increases blood flow, relieves tension, boosts the immune system, increases oxygen flow, among other benefits. And, it feels good! If you don't have a massage therapist, find one and schedule an appointment this week.

Caregiver Pledge:

To care for myself, I pledge to exercise at least 3 times a week for at least 20 minutes. And, I promise to schedule at least one massage.

Summary

❖ **Take Time** to exercise for physical and mental health.

❖ **Stress Hormones** are secreted during times of high stress and exercise encourages the body back to a state of relaxation.

❖ **Stress Relief and Strength** through exercise helps you be mentally clearer and more physically able to keep up with changes in the person you care for.

❖ **Exercise Suggestions** include walking, weight training, dancing, pilates or yoga.

❖ **Get Out of the House** if possible for a change of scenery and fresh air.

❖ **Massage** has therapeutic benefit by helping the lymphatic system move toxins out of the body, increasing blood flow, relieving tension, boosting the immune system and it feels great.

❖ For additional information, please visit,
*http://www.HopeForCaregivers.com/**exercise***

ME TIME (3)

BREATHING

Best Bet to Relax? Breathe!

Pay Attention:

Your body breathes naturally—with or without your attention, however, you can affect your body by paying attention to *how* you are breathing.

Short, Shallow Breathing:

I'll bet if you take a moment to notice, you will discover that you take lots of short, shallow breaths. The more stressful your situation, the more you tend to take short, shallow breaths.

Oxygen:

Oxygen is necessary for health and breathing is the chief way you take it in. Oxygen is required for the proper operation of all body systems. It not only helps to detoxify the body, it's also essential for strengthening the immune system.

Stress Effects:

Stress and health are closely linked. Either quick or constant stress can induce issues in the body or the mind. Clear thinking is only possible by assisting your body with an adequate intake of oxygen. With a prolonged stressful state, your body may express anxiety, tension, dizzy spells, sleeplessness or nervousness, among other things.

Relaxation Breathing:

One of the ways to ensure that you are taking in oxygen and giving yourself a chance to return to a more relaxed state is by deep breathing. Try the following cycle of breathing 2 or 3 times. Your goal is to complete 5 cycles. Sometimes an increased intake of oxygen (when you normally breathe in a shallow manner) can leave you feeling lightheaded. As with anything new, approach with care.

- ❀ Place one hand over your abdomen and feel the belly move as you breathe. Your hand should rise and fall as you inhale and exhale.

- ❀ Exhale completely.

- ❀ Count in your mind as you do the following:

- ❀ Breathe in as you count to 4.

- ❀ Hold the breath for a count of 7.

- ❀ Exhale, completely, for a count of 8.

Caregiver Pledge:

I promise to practice relaxation breathing every day. The more stress I feel, the more I will pay attention to my breathing.

Summary

- ❀ **Pay Attention** to your breathing.

- ❀ **Short, Shallow Breathing** is common in stressful situations.

- ❀ **Oxygen** is essential for health as it detoxifies the body as well as strengthens the immune system.

- ❀ **Stress Effects** due to a prolonged stressful state include increased anxiety, tension, dizzy spells, sleeplessness and nervousness may be helped by good breathing technique.

- ❀ **Relaxation Breathing** means inhale for 4, hold for 7, and exhale for 8 and repeat.

- ❀ For additional information please visit, *http://www.HopeForCaregivers.com/**breathing***

ME TIME (4)

SUPPORT GROUPS

Support — a Lifesaver

Burnout:

The longer the caregiving journey lasts, the more overwhelming and lonely it becomes and the greater the chance for burnout. One of the ways to stave off caregiver burnout is to join a support group.

Finding Support:

Speaking from my own experience, finding a caregivers' support group was a lifesaver for me. The monthly meetings were devoted to specific aspects of caregiving, enabling me to provide better care for my parents. Topics ranged from wound care to navigating the Medicare maze, selecting an assisted living facility and what to look for when choosing a nursing home. The group I attended met at a local hospital and was facilitated by several nurses. As they are professional caregivers, nurses understand both the needs of the caregiver and the patient.

Support Group Benefit:

Another benefit I found with the in-person support group was a connection with other caregivers who understood the path I was traveling. Knowing I was not the only person who felt stressed and overwhelmed, somehow made my journey more tolerable.

Online Support:

If you find it impossible to participate in a live support group, check online groups. I'll bet you can find a fitting group, regardless of how specific your situation is. Once you find a group, you can choose to read about others' experiences or you may wish to participate in discussions. And, if you don't agree with someone, simply use the power of your delete key.

Caregiver Pledge:

I pledge to find a support group. No matter how long I've been a caregiver, I realize that I need support. By interacting with others who understand the path I'm walking, I will be a better caregiver.

Summary

❀ **Burnout** occurs when the caregiver is overwhelmed, exhausted and lonely.

❀ **Finding Support** can be challenging but worth the effort in assisting the caregiver with information and understanding.

❀ **Support Group** benefits are individual yet provide an important sense of community.

❀ **Online Support** is available for most specific caregiving situations.

❀ For additional information please visit, http://www.HopeForCaregivers.com/**support-groups**

ME TIME (5)

GARDENING

Get Dirty and Grow Something!

Plants:

Plants don't ask for much. They need some light, water, decent soil and a little fertilizer. In return they produce flowers or food or simply adorn your environment. (A side benefit—they don't talk to you! A few moments of silence in the middle of a hectic day—bliss!)

Container Gardening:

If you can get outside and dig in the dirt, it's good for your body as well as your soul. Playing in the dirt helps keep you grounded. If you don't have the opportunity or space to create a garden, why not try container gardening? A plain terra cotta pot or two filled with herbs or fragrant blooms can supply you with beauty and a little aroma therapy which can have a remarkably soothing effect on the spirit. Search the Internet, buy a magazine or check out a book from the library where you can learn about combining plants, whether they are bedding plants, vegetable plants, herbs or a combination.

Slow Down:

Enjoy the process of slowing down long enough to feel the soil sift through your fingers. Smell the aroma of the earth. Notice the colors of the seeds, foliage and blooms. If you garden without pressure, the potential reward is tremendous.

Caregiver Pledge:

I pledge to carve out some time every week to play in the dirt. I promise to plant at least one pot of flowers or other plants. I might even try a little garden.

Summary

- ❃ **Plants** don't need much to be happy and they provide much needed beauty as well as silence in the midst of a crazy day.

- ❃ **Container Gardening** is an easy, time-efficient way to enjoy plants.

- ❃ **Slow Down** and enjoy the process.

- ❃ For additional information please visit. *http://www.HopeForCaregivers.com/gardening*

ME TIME (6)

JOURNALING

Write, Draw, Paste or Doodle

Caregiving Journal:

Before you say, "I can't" or "I don't have time," please take a deep breath and just try it. Some caregivers find journaling essential for tracking changes in the person they care for. If you record changes in behavior, mobility, appetite, etc., you will have specific information to take to medical appointments. For this type of journaling, be sure to note a date, time of day and your observations. Note—If you like working on your computer, there are programs available that guide you through notations with a small investment of your time.

Appreciation Journal:

Another type of journaling I suggest is creating a gratitude or appreciation journal. Pick up a blank book or an inexpensive composition notebook for your writing. Promise yourself to jot down 3 to 5 things every day that you are grateful for. List the things that went well on a given day. Also, be appreciative of yourself. List what you have done well. Give yourself compliments. As you express your feelings of gratitude, your energy changes and helps you discover a more positive attitude as caregiving responsibilities threaten to deplete you.

Art Journal:

Art or visual journaling can provide a super way to express yourself with or without words. Scribbling or sketching with a new box of crayons, colored pencils or inexpensive watercolors is a wonderful thing to do. Use colors you like or those that seem to express the way you feel. There are no rules. Just do it! And, if you don't feel confident in drawing or doodling, cut or tear out magazine images and glue them into your journal. Then, you can write or doodle around the images, if you like. Or, tear the images into small pieces and divide into color groups. Just pretend to "paint" with the pieces of paper by gluing them into your journal. Express yourself and play.

Caregiver Pledge:

Today I promise to find a journal and I will enjoy a few minutes every day to write or doodle or glue stuff into it. I promise myself that I will play. I deserve it!

Summary

❀ **Caregiving Journal** is the place to make notes and track changes in the person you care for.

❀ **Appreciation Journal** is the place to write your gratitude list and things that **you** have done well.

❀ **Art Journal** is the place to play with crayons, pencils, paints, words, and images. There are no rules. Express yourself and enjoy the process.

❀ For additional information please visit.
*http://www.HopeForCaregivers.com/**journaling***

ME TIME (7)

PUT YOURSELF IN TIMEOUT

Timeout Staves-off Burnout

Stop and Refuel:
   Please know that caring for someone else is a balancing act. You must find the balance between caring for your loved one and caring for yourself. Without that balance, your longevity as a caregiver is going to be short-lived. Steal a few moments to be calm and refuel yourself. Time Out!

   Stop doing anything. You could spend some time breathing or perhaps a few moments in meditation. Amazingly, even just five or ten minutes of silence can really refresh you. Both relaxation breathing and meditation have positive effects on the mind as well as the body. Or, use your time for prayer. Ask for help or express your gratitude for strength and stamina to continue your caregiving journey.

Put Your Feet Up:
   If meditation and prayer don't resonate with you, just sit. That's right. Sit. Put your feet up and don't worry about the list scrolling through your mind. Somehow, things wait.

Timeout or Burnout:

If you don't take timeout, you will burnout. Signs of burnout include, fuzzy thinking, anxiety, depression, not being able to sleep, lack of appetite, and becoming easily angered, to name a few. Caregiver burnout threatens the well-being of almost every caregiver. So, rather than burnout, take a timeout!

Caregiver Pledge:

I pledge to put myself in Timeout. I accept the fact that for me to be able to care for someone else, I must take time for myself. At least once every day, I will find moments to meditate, pray....

or simply sit.

Summary

❀ **Stop and Refuel** by putting yourself in timeout.

❀ **Put Your Feet Up** and let the world wait for a while.

❀ **Timeout or Burnout** are your two choices. If you don't take some time for yourself, burnout is guaranteed. Timeout is definitely a better choice.

❀ For additional information please visit,
http://www.HopeForCaregivers.com/__timeout__

ME TIME (8)

HOBBIES

Creativity Feeds the Soul

Creativity:

Quite by accident I discovered a new hobby. I had been actively caregiving for several years when I found it. I am a creative person by nature and not having the blocks of time to feed my creative self caused me to feel like my soul was shriveling.

Find a Hobby:

I found my new hobby—making jewelry—when I was looking for something on the Internet. I was intrigued and decided to give it a try. I began simply at first, not caring about my success. I just needed to use my hands to create something. Everything fit on a lap tray, allowing me to easily pick it up, work on a new piece or just play when time allowed.

Sense of Accomplishment:

When I finished a piece of jewelry, I admired my work. I held it in my hand and marveled at the result of a few minutes here or there. I loved having something that said, "Look! You did it!" Although I never regretted caring for my mom, much of what I did had to be redone within hours or days—laundry, ordering and organizing medications, fixing every meal, doing the dishes, etc. Having something finished that stayed finished provided a much needed sense of accomplishment.

Play Often:

I strongly suggest that you find something to do that stays done—something that you can hold in your hand. Learn to play with polymer clay, create a scrapbook, string beads, cross stitch, doodle in the form of zentangling, use rubber stamps or punches to decorate or alter a book. Use your imagination and make something.

Caregiver Pledge:

I pledge to spend a few minutes at least twice a week playing with a hobby.

Summary

- **Creativity** feeds the soul.
- **Find a Hobby**, old or new, and enjoy it.
- **Sense of Accomplishment** is important for the caregiver because you can finish something that stays finished.
- **Play Often** and use your imagination.
- For additional information please visit, http://www.HopeForCaregivers.com/**hobbies**

ME TIME (9)

RITUALS

Rituals Keep You Centered

Childhood Rituals:

My parents and I attended a large church from the moment my mother felt it was safe "to take the baby out in public." Our church was resplendent in it's beautiful sanctuary and countless rituals. Growing up, the rituals were normal to me until I became a teenager when they felt stilted and something I thought people used as masks. Part of growing into adulthood is questioning everything. Although I didn't know it at the time, my rebellion against ritual allowed me to stretch my wings to explore other faiths and ways to view the world.

Life Happens:

Years passed and I married, raised a family and became a caregiver. During the first few weeks of caregiving, ritual reentered my life, but not within a church.

A New Ritual:

To connect with each other, my husband and I began meeting every afternoon for a simple cup of coffee. Although most of our afternoon rendezvous involved coffee, the ritual of stopping—no matter what—and spending time together was the most important thing. The daily break became truly sacred to us, just as the rituals I remembered from church, were sacred to the congregants.

Ritual Means Comfort:

I learned through our coffee dates that ritual meant comfort. It was something I could count on. It helped keep me centered. Looking back I'm certain that such a simple ritual helped me maintain my sanity.

Caregiver Pledge:

I pledge to identify at least one ritual. I will do my utmost to honor the sacredness of my ritual and will reserve that time to care for myself.

Summary

- ❀ **Childhood Rituals** may be comforting or something you rebel against.

- ❀ **Life Happens** and rituals change.

- ❀ **A New Ritual** may be very unexpected.

- ❀ **Ritual Means Comfort** and something you can count on while helping to keep you centered.

- ❀ For additional information please visit, *http://www.HopeForCaregivers.com/**rituals***

ME TIME (10)

READING

Read While You Wait

Information:

You can never have too much information. Whether reading books, information you find on the Internet, magazines, or source material that specifically deals with your caregiving situation, just keep reading. Even if you're not an avid reader, you need information. By purchasing a CD player or a device such as an iPod, you can listen to the books instead of having to physically read them.

Waiting:

Most caregiving situations involve a lot of waiting. You wait for doctors. You wait in hospitals. You wait for prescriptions to be filled. You wait for people to return calls. You wait to see how the person you are caring for responds to something — a new medication, a change in behavior, etc. Each of these situations provides a great opportunity to spend some time reading or listening. Take advantage of them.

One Word or One Technique:

You can always learn something that might make your caregiving experience less stressful. Sometimes one word or one technique can provide enough relief to keep you moving forward.

Caregiver Pledge:

I promise to stay open to new information

to help me and the person I care for,

no matter where I find it.

Summary

✾ **Information** comes from many sources. Stay open. Read, listen, or both whenever you have the opportunity.

✾ **Waiting** provides a great time to read. Always have something to read.

✾ **One Word or One Technique** picked up while reading can be exactly what you need to keep you going.

✾ For additional information please visit, *http://www.HopeForCaregivers.com/**reading***

ME TIME (11)

UNCONDITIONAL LOVE

Nothing Feels as Good as Unconditional Love

Pets:

I have lived with at least one animal from the day I came into this world. At first there were our milk goats, then a Boxer puppy that became my constant companion along with various kittens and cats. Each of them provided me with a special, unspoken connection to love and acceptance. I cannot imagine living without the unconditional love and comfort that each of them has so willingly shared with me.

When my mom moved in with us, we were already living with with two cats and a dog. Mom brought her cat with her and six months later, we acquired a rescued puppy. While caring for my rapidly aging mother, three cats and two dogs could have been the end of my sanity!

An Unexpected Asset:

Instead, our new puppy, who needed much assurance that being alive could be a great adventure, provided an excuse for me to spend time giving and receiving unconditional love. She helped me stay anchored to a somewhat normal life as I watched her explore her new world. In spite of her puppy antics and much needed training, I never questioned the timing or regretted our new family member.

If you have the opportunity to enjoy a pet, I encourage you to do so.

Alternatives:

Maybe in your situation you can't have a pet. Shelters everywhere need help. You could volunteer to walk a dog or assist in the shelter. By giving a dog or cat, waiting for a forever home, a good day, you just might be the recipient of some of that amazing unconditional love. Give it some thought.

Caregiver Pledge:

I pledge to willingly receive the unconditional love provided by animals who come into my life.

Summary

❀ **Pets** willingly provide unconditional love.

❀ **An Unexpected Asset** may come from a surprising situation. Keep your heart and your arms open.

❀ **Alternatives** might include volunteering at a shelter. Be open to opportunities and embrace the reward.

❀ For additional information please visit,
*http://www.HopeForCaregivers.com/**pets***

ME TIME (12)

PEACE & QUIET

Peace Restores Balance

Peace and Quiet:

As a caregiver, the only time in my day void of responsibility was late evening. When everyone was finally sleeping, I felt a wonderful sense of peace. Peace and quiet…ahhhhh…time to breathe…time to do whatever I wanted to do without doing anything for anyone else. I didn't have to plan anything, go anywhere, or be responsible.

For me, if my choice was trying to sleep (which I found very challenging) or spending an hour or two alone, I chose the latter. My alone time was almost as refreshing as sleep. Sometimes I read or worked on a hobby. Sometimes I watched television or videos on the computer. The activity was of little importance, but the time free of responsibility was crucial to maintaining my sanity.

Find Your Time:

Not since my years in college have I been a morning person. But, perhaps you are. If so, maybe that's when you can grab some alone time.

The point is, you—the caregiver—need some time for yourself. You don't need to justify it, either. It's a fact. Everyone needs some off-duty, down time.

Try various options until you find those moments that belong to you and no one else. Enjoy your time. It's yours and you deserve every minute of it!!

Caregiver Pledge:

I pledge to take time just for me. It is important for me to be alone, responsible for nothing.

Summary

- ❀ **Peace and Quiet** means doing anything you want to do for yourself and enjoying a lack of responsibility.

- ❀ **Find Your Time** whether daylight or dark. Whatever the time, take advantage of being off duty. Relax.

- ❀ For additional information please visit, *http://www.HopeForCaregivers.com/peace*

ME TIME

CAREGIVER PLEDGES

Here's the place to begin taking care of yourself. I certainly don't have all the answers as, even today, my healing and self-care continue to be a bit of a struggle. Some days you will be more successful than others at finding some **Me Time**. The point is not perfection, it is knowing that you are worth it. You are not only worth it, you are entitled to it.

To remind you, here they are again. Remember, take the caregiver's pledges. You'll be a much more effective caregiver if you do.

❀ I pledge to **nourish** my body by eating the best foods because I am worth it.

❀ To care for myself, I pledge to **exercise** at least 3 times a week for at least 20 minutes. And, I promise to schedule a massage.

❀ I promise to practice relaxation **breathing** every day. The more stress I feel, the more I will pay attention to my breathing.

❀ I pledge to find a **support group**. No matter how long I've been a caregiver, I realize that I need support. By interacting with others who understand the path I'm walking, I will be a better caregiver.

❀ I pledge to carve out some time every week to **play in the dirt**. I promise to plant at least one pot of flowers or other plants. I might even try a little garden.

❀ Today I promise to find a **journal** and I will enjoy a few minutes every day to write or doodle or glue stuff into it. I promise myself that I will play. I deserve it!

❀ I pledge to put myself in **Timeout**. I accept the fact that for me to be able to care for someone else, I must take time for myself. At least once every day, I will find moments to meditate, pray or simply sit.

❀ I pledge to spend a few minutes at least twice a week playing with a **hobby**.

❀ I pledge to identify at least one **ritual**. I will do my utmost to honor the sacredness of my ritual and will reserve that time to care for myself.

❀ I promise to stay open to **new information** to help me and the person I care for, no matter where I find it.

❀ I pledge to willingly receive the **unconditional love** provided by animals who come into my life.

❀ I pledge to take **time just for me**. It is important for me to be alone, responsible for nothing.

There you have it—a few ideas to help you figure out how to take care of yourself. Always remember, you deserve it.

I survived the caregiving experience... you can, too.

EPILOGUE

My caregiving roller coaster ride eventually ended. There was no way for me to foresee the twists and turns it would take, yet through it all, I managed to keep my eyes open and stare down the fear of losing people I loved. Our time together, once seemingly endless, came to a close. I have survived and been given a renewed purpose for my life.

Through it all, I discovered one undeniable truth. My life is deeper and richer than before the journey began. I greet every day with anticipation and joy as my life is once again filled with art, music, flowers, and teaching. My husband and I still celebrate our afternoon coffee dates, often remembering my mother joining us. He and I join forces in artistic adventures in our studio as we work together in gratitude for each other and the world around us. My son, now an amazing man who continues to design a life that I never dared to dream, insisted that I share my caregiving journey with the world. Because of his vision and coaxing, I'm sharing this story with you.

Looking back over the years devoted to my parents, I have no regret. I cared for the people who gave me life just as they cared for me as a helpless baby, small child, confused teenager and willful young adult. I am grateful for each experience and lesson, no matter how isolated and lonely I felt.

No longer encumbered by overwhelming responsibility, I am free to pursue my life. I feel whole again, but with much greater understanding and compassion for those who care for others. There really is a circle of life, and I am truly blessed by choosing to participate in it!

Dear Reader,

If you find yourself in the role of caregiver, in my heart I share your burden. You are doing one of the most challenging jobs in Earth school. Some days aren't so hard to manage and others are impossible. Please know that you are not alone. Every day thousands and thousands of people are actively caregiving. I urge you to look for support and resources beyond yourself. They are available, and you need each and every one you find. Although I don't know you personally, with all my heart, I send you love and energy. And, please remember that when you have done everything that you know to do, sometimes you just have to be still and wait. Answers will appear and if you can just hang on, you will survive. Your life will never be the same as before assuming the caregiving role, but it can be better. Each day is a gift because it is fresh and new. In spirit, I am walking with you. You are not alone.

ONE LAST THING

This book, based on my journals, spanned several years. It was an evolutionary project and essential for my own healing process. At first, my writings were just a record of the day to day events because I needed some way to measure how things were changing for me and my parents. As the demands of the caregiving journey increased, entries in my journal were sometimes interrupted for long periods, leaving holes in my memory. As I began actively writing the story, details slowly began to fill the gaps. When one of them appeared, I couldn't imagine how I'd forgotten it.

Then I remembered a conversation with one of my life-teachers when he spoke about the old country stores and their pickle barrels. In order to preserve cucumbers, they were submerged in brine inside a large barrel. If a pickled cucumber surfaced and was left alone, it would become rancid and spoil the rest. He went on to explain that long forgotten events and memories could float up in the mind, just like the pickles that needed attention. I began to understand that my conscious mind, occupied by the pressure of our daily routine, apparently let go of many details.

As time passed and the stress lessened, memories safely floated to the surface of my "pickle barrel" where I could address, accept and heal them.

I suspect that some pickles might still be waiting to rise up. When they do, I'll write about them on my blog at _www.HopeForCaregivers.com_. I hope you can join me there as together we continue on the path of hope and healing.

ACKNOWLEDGMENTS

This story, based on my caregiving journey, would have existed only in journals and my mind without the support of many people for whom I am truly grateful.

To all the active caregivers who took their valuable time to read this story and who encouraged me to get it out to the world to help others, thank you.

To my support system of friends who never ceased loving and standing with me, thank you.

To my truly amazing son, who tirelessly believed in this project and figured out the way to make it reality, thank you.

To my husband, who stood beside me without wavering through the grieving and healing process, as well as the craziness of writing this story, thank you.

To my G.A.L.S. (Grief and Life Support group) who witnessed my gaping wounds, held me up during my rawest moments and walked with me toward a new life, thank you.

And where would I be without my mother?

She inspires me every single day.

Thank you!

∽ ∽ ♡ ∽ ∽

ABOUT THE AUTHOR

Without her knowledge, Barb Owen fit the exact profile of today's caregiver. Life was flowing along for her as a wife, mother, daughter, grandmother and artist. Barb didn't have any idea that life could change in a heartbeat with the collision between her life and that of the caregiver.

As a wife of more than 35 years, she was enjoying life with her husband, alone, for the very first time.

Nothing in Barb's life was more important to her than being a wife, mother and grandmother. Nurturing and encouraging came first.

Barb began pursuing artistic avenues at a young age and included everything from music to working with paper, fiber, fabric and metal. Teaching music at the age of 16 ignited her lifelong passion of inspiring others to trust their creative spirits.

Just as her life was settling into a nice rhythm, balanced between husband, adult children and artistic ventures, the role of caregiver interrupted, stalling everything. Her parents were in crisis. Her siblings were terrified. And, everyone looked to her to take the helm.

Today, Barb encourages caregivers through her website *www.HopeForCaregivers.com* and is once again enjoying her life with abandon.

SUGGESTED READING FOR CAREGIVERS

As I emphasized in the Me Time section on reading, as a caregiver, you can never have too much information. You will glean ideas from lots of sources and even if you only find one suggestion that makes life easier, it's worth reading. Personally, I read everything with a pen in hand. I marked anything that stood out to me and often made notes in a special journal so that I didn't have to continually refer back to the original text. My journal provided me with a condensed version of all the books I'd read about caregiving as they applied to our specific situation.

Below you will find a list of books that I found particularly helpful. Keep your eyes open and never assume that you have all the answers. The caregiving experience is as varied as the people involved. Keep reading.

Books about Caregiving:
- **Eldercare for Dummies,** by Dr. Rachelle Zuker
- **The Fearless Caregiver**, by Gary Barg
- **Caregiving**, by Beth Witrogen McLeod
- **The 36-Hour Day**, by Mace and Rabins
- **Caregivers' Comfort**, by Julie Cook Downing
- **Share the Care**, by Capossela Warnock

Books about Death and Dying:
- **Final Gifts**, by Callanan and Kelley
- **Life Lessons**, by Ross and Kessler
- **The Needs of the Dying**, by Kessler
- **The Dying Time**, by Furman and McNabb

Books on Grief and Recovery After Caregiving:

- **Seven Choices**, by Elizabeth Harper Neeld
- **The Grief Recovery Handbook**, by James and Friedman
- **Chicken Soup for the Grieving Soul**, by Canfield and Hansen
- **The Sedona Method**, by Hale Dwoskin
- **Visual Journaling: Going Deeper than Words**, by Ganin and Fox

Books to Encourage:

- **14,000 Things to be Happy About**, by Workman
- **Relax - 200 Ways to Achieve Calm in Mind and Body**, by Renata & Steven Ash

◎◎◎

All of the above are available at their respective outlets or may be purchsed through;
http://www.HopeForCaregivers.com/giftshop

◎◎◎

We hope you enjoyed this HopeForCaregivers.com book.
If you'd like to receive updates on future books, products or if
you'd like information about the author, please;

Contact Us

T&T1 inc.
PO Box 30716
Columbia, MO 65205-3716
(573) 723-1510

www.HopeForCaregivers.com
contact@HopeForCaregivers.com

www.NormalDoesntLiveHereAnymore.com
contact@NormalDoesntLiveHereAnymore.com

Published and distributed worldwide by: T&T1 inc.,
PO Box 30716, Columbia, MO 65205-3716 • Phone: (573) 723-1510

Be sure to visit **HopeForCaregivers.com** and enjoy the
best inspirational messages of hope and encouragment for the
caregiving comunity! And, sign up at the website for a special
FREE GIFT and newsletter to stay informed about what's going
on with the caregiver support comunity. You are not alone. Just
keep putting one foot in front of the other. You WILL survive.

www.HopeForCaregivers.com

Made in the USA
Charleston, SC
01 June 2011